W9-BTM-417

OFFICIAL LITTLE LEAGUE BASEBALL® RULES IN PICTURES

Introduction by Dr. Creighton J. Hale
President and CEO, Little League Baseball®

Illustrated by Phil Perez,
Manny Campana, and Michael Brown

A PERIGEE BOOK

Perigee Books
are published by
The Putnam Publishing Group
200 Madison Avenue
New York, NY 10016

Library of Congress Cataloging-in-Publication Data

Official Little League Baseball® rules in pictures / introduction by
Creighton J. Hale; illustrated by Phil Perez, Manny Campana, and
Michael Brown.

p. cm.
Reprint. Originally published: New York: Grosset & Dunlap, c1979.
1. Little League Baseball, inc. 2. Baseball—Rules. I. Perez,
Phil. II. Campana, Manny. III. Brown, Michael, IV. Title: Little
League Baseball rules in pictures.
[GV877.045   1989]   88-32449 CIP
796.357′62—dc19
ISBN 0-399-51531-3

Printed in the United States of America
6   7   8   9   10

INTRODUCTION

To transform the *Little League Baseball Rule Book* into a clear, easy-to-understand, pictorial publication might seem like a dream come true for Little League enthusiasts throughout the world. Out of necessity, the compact, pocket-size rule book published by Little League Baseball® might seem forbidding to some, with its pages of technical interpretations and lack of visual examples.

In this book, *Official Little League Baseball Rules in Pictures,* the resulting void has been filled so perfectly that this publication is a natural companion to the *Little League Baseball Rule Book* and should be the foundation of every Little League library. Troublesome playing situations with appropriate rulings are presented in visual form for easy comprehension by all. The actual Little League rules are also presented for quick reference and further understanding.

Its usefulness to managers, coaches, umpires, and other adults is apparent. However, of more importance is its appeal to participants in Little League Baseball. For the over two million youngsters who play in the Little League every year, *Little League Baseball Rules in Pictures* will provide—for perhaps the first time—a very readable publication for their own understanding and appreciation of the rules by which they play.

We heartily recommend this book. As a tool for better understanding the rules of Little League Baseball, it is a tremendous asset.

C. J. HALE
President and CEO
Little League Baseball

A. Coacher's box, 4′ × 8′; 6′ from the foul line

B. Next batter's circle, 3′ in diameter and 10′ from the dugout

C. Dugout, 20′ long

D. Protective fence, 6′ high

E. Fence, 30″ high with wire screen 8′ above (28′ optional distance from the foul line)

F. Back stop (20′ optional distance from the rear of home plate)

G. 18′ circle

H. Fence, 2′6″ to 3′ high

I. Foul line, 200′ optional

J. Recommended outfield fence, 4′ high (height and distance from home plate optional)

K. Scoreboard

L. Flag pole

M. Optional outfield fence, 200′ from "point" of home plate

N. Pitcher's mound, 10′ circle

O. 50′ radius from pitching plate

P. 84′10″ from "point" of home plate

Q. 60′

R. 9′ radius from farthest point of base

THE FIELD AND EQUIPMENT

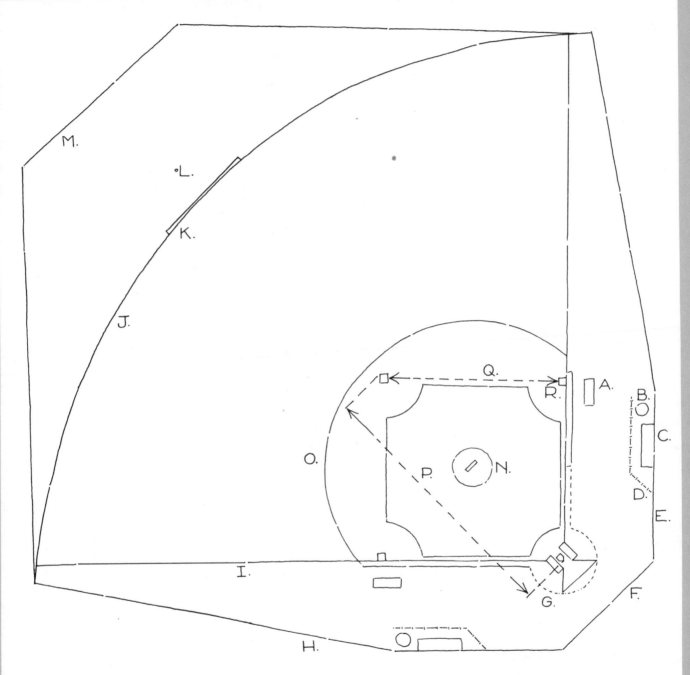

This is a drawing of a Little League Baseball field. The size and shape of all the important parts must be as the rules say (rule 1.04).

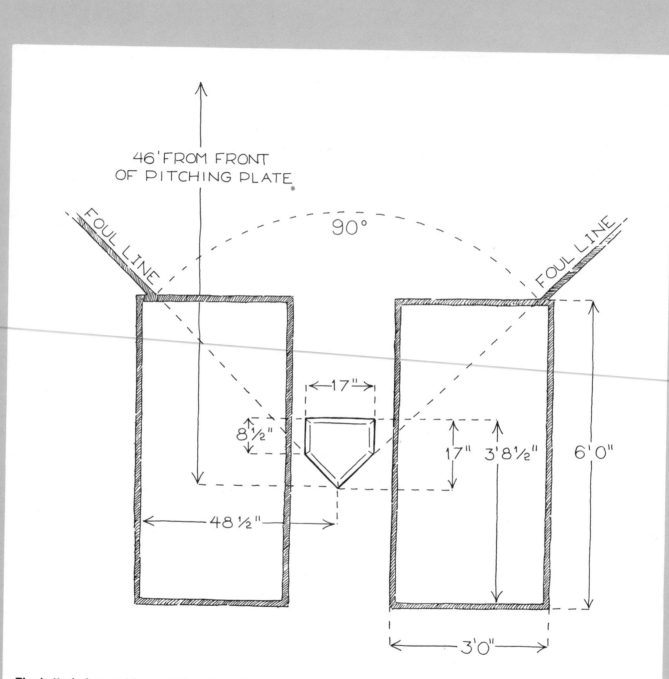

The batter's box and home plate (rules 1.04 and 1.05).

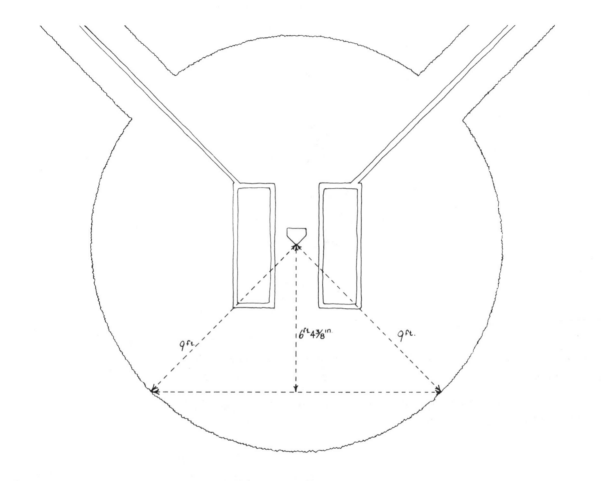

The catcher's box. It is made by continuing the foul lines back beyond home plate (rule 1.04).

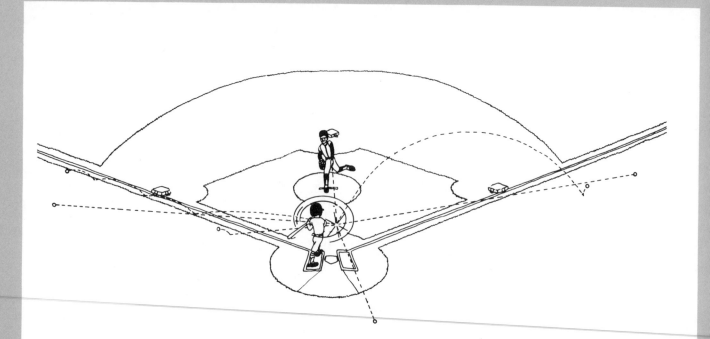

The batter has hit six foul balls. Foul territory is the part of the field outside the first and third baselines all the way out to and straight up to the top of the outfield fence.

Fair territory is the part of the field inside those lines. The baselines and the bases are part of fair territory (rule 2.00).

All the players on one team should wear the same uniform (rule 1.11a).

The Official Little League Shoulder Patch should be put on the left shoulder (rule 1.11a).

The rules say which size and type of equipment may be used—for example, a first base glove may be only so big; plastic or rubber cleats may be used, but not metal ones (rules 1.11–1.17).

The league should have enough batting helmets for the batter, the on-deck batter, the baserunners, and the coaches. The players must use them (rule 1.16).

HOW THE GAME IS PLAYED

After the teams have taken their places, nine members of the home team in the field and a member of the visiting team at bat, the umpire will call "Play!" The game has **started** (rule 4.02).

The pitcher tries to pitch the ball past the batter, who may choose to swing at it or **not** (rule 2.00: A Strike; rule 5.03).

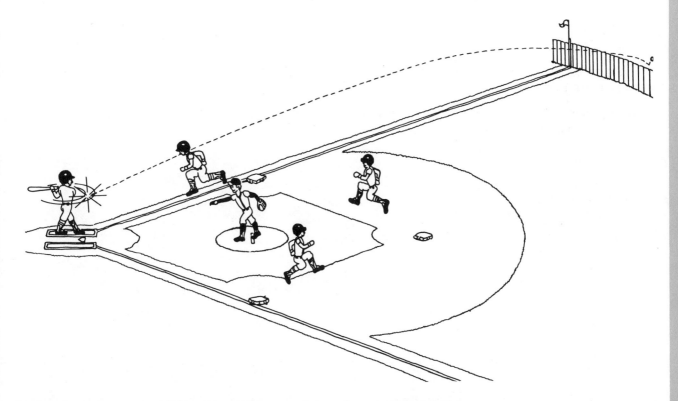

If the batter hits a fair ball, the batter becomes a baserunner and will try to touch base. When the batter touches all the bases, a run is **scored** (rule 4.09).

This is a double play. The team in the field is putting the batter and the other baserunner out (rule 2.00).

When any three batters or baserunners are put out, the team in the field gets its turn at bat and the batting team moves into the field (rule 5.07).

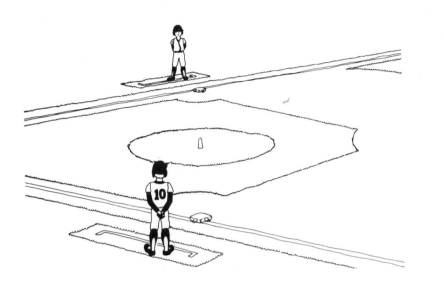

During the game, the manager is in charge of the team. The coachers help the manager by signaling to the runners or the batter from the coachers' boxes (rules 2.00 and 4.05).

The plate umpire is in charge of the other umpires and stands behind the catcher. This person's official title is Umpire-in-Chief (rule 9.04).

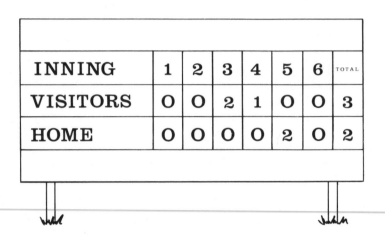

INNING	1	2	3	4	5	6	TOTAL
VISITORS	0	0	2	1	0	0	3
HOME	0	0	0	0	2	0	2

Each team bats until three of its players are out. An inning is completed when both teams have been to bat and made three outs. A regulation game is six innings long.

If a game is tied after six innings, extra innings will be played. The game will end when one team is ahead at the end of an inning (rules 4.10–4.11).

THE BATTER'S BOX

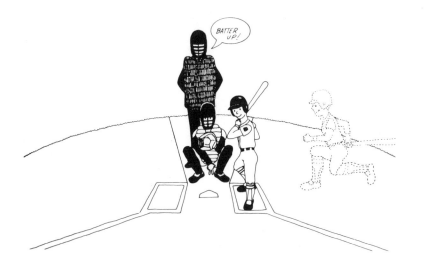

When the umpire calls the batter, the batter should come promptly and get ready to hit (rule 6.02).

The batter should have both feet inside the batter's box. Feet on the line count as being inside the box (rule 6.03).

If the batter hits the ball while a foot is all the way outside the batter's box, the batter is out (rules 2.00 and 6.06a).

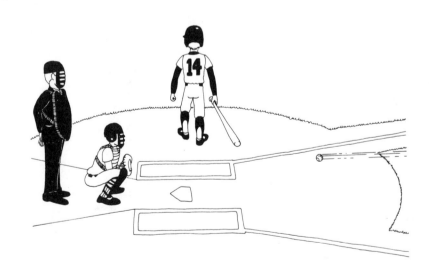

The batter may not leave the batter's box when the pitcher is in a "set" or "windup" position. The pitch will count, whether it's a ball or a strike (6.02b).

If the batter steps from one batter's box to another when the pitcher is in a set or windup position, the batter is out (rule 6.06b).

WHEN IS THE BATTER OUT?

HERE ARE THE TWO MOST COMMON WAYS A BATTER MAY BE PUT OUT:

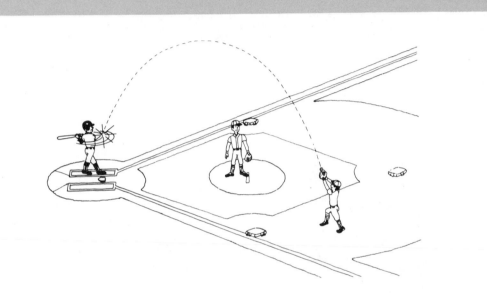

1) When the batter hits a fair or foul fly ball, if a fielder catches it the batter is out (rule 6.05a).

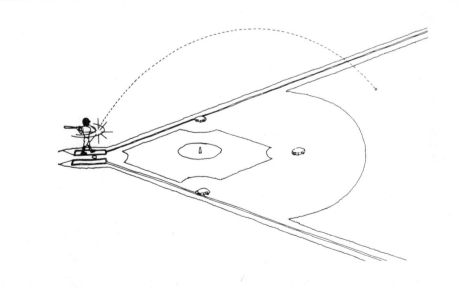

A fly ball is a ball batted high into the air (rule 2.00).

2) The batter is out if three strikes are called. It doesn't matter if the third strike is caught by the catcher or dropped (rule 6.05).

STRIKES

A STRIKE IS USUALLY CALLED FOR ONE OF THREE REASONS:

1) A strike is a pitch that the batter tries to hit and misses (rule 2.00).

2) If any part of a pitched ball passes through any part of the strike zone and the batter doesn't try to hit it, it's a strike (rule 2.00).

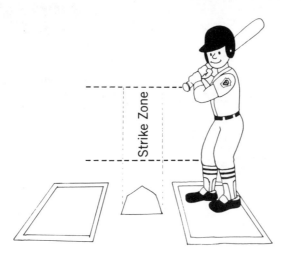

The strike zone is the area over home plate beginning at the batter's knees and reaching to the batter's armpits, when the batter is standing in a natural bat-swinging position (rule 2.00).

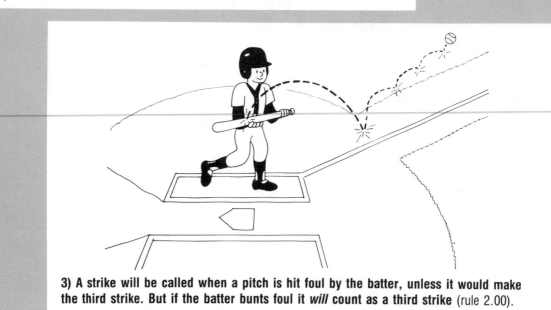

3) A strike will be called when a pitch is hit foul by the batter, unless it would make the third strike. But if the batter bunts foul it *will* count as a third strike (rule 2.00).

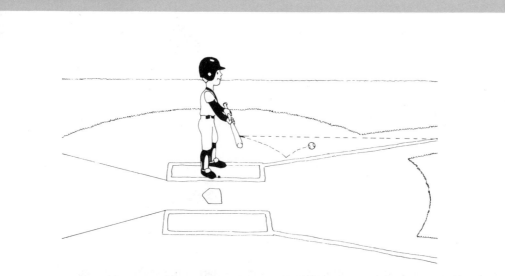

A bunt is a batted ball not swung at but tapped softly so it won't go far (rule 2.00).

A strike will be called if a pitch touches the batter in the strike zone (rule 2.00).

A strike will be called if the batter is touched by the ball while swinging at it (rule 2.00).

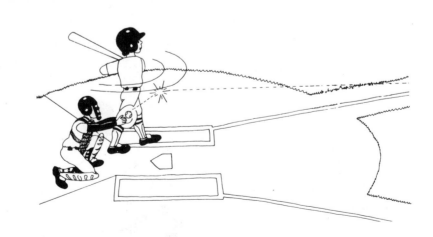

If a ball is fouled straight back to the catcher, who catches it, the batter is not out. A strike is called. The ball stays in play. This is called a foul tip (rule 2.00).

SOME OTHER REASONS A BATTER IS CALLED OUT:

The batter will be called out if, after hitting a fair ball, the batter is hit by the ball before a fielder has had a chance to make a play (rule 6.05g).

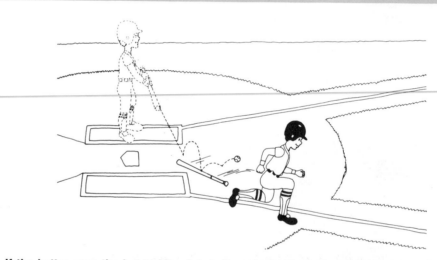

If the batter uses the bat to hit a fair ball a second time, the batter will be out (rule 6.05h).

But if the bat has been dropped and the umpire thinks that the batter did not mean to hit the ball a second time, the batter is not out and the play goes on (rule 6.05h).

This batter is called out for interfering with the catcher, who is trying to make a play (rule 6.06).

If an infield fly is called by the umpire, or the umpire thinks a fielder let a ball drop on purpose to set up a force play, the batter is out (rules 2.00 and 6.05L).

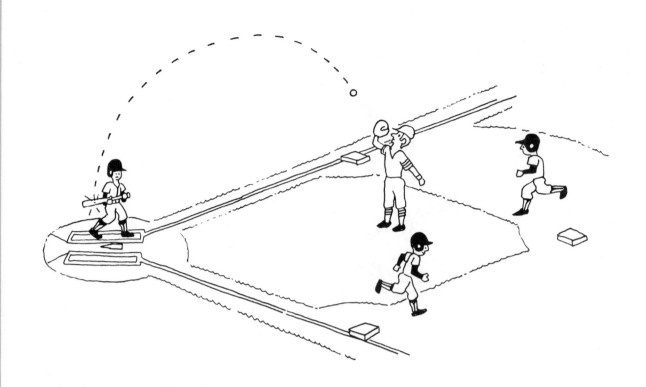

A bunted ball is not an infield fly (rule 2.00).

A batter will be out if a baserunner touches a batted ball on purpose or interferes with a fielder trying to play the ball. The runner will be out, too (rule 7.09g).

A batter will be called out if a teammate takes and *completes* that batter's turn at bat. The manager of the other team must point this out to the umpire before the next play begins (rule 6.07a).

WHEN THE BATTER BECOMES A BASERUNNER

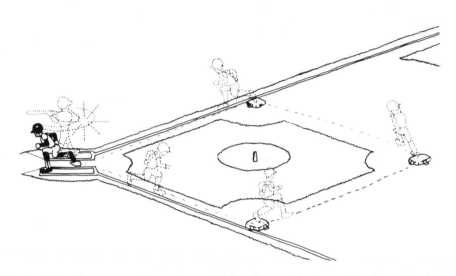

When the batter becomes a baserunner and touches all the bases legally, a run is **scored** (rule 5.06).

HERE ARE SOME WAYS A BATTER BECOMES A BASERUNNER:

The batter becomes a baserunner when a fair ball is hit (rule 6.09a).

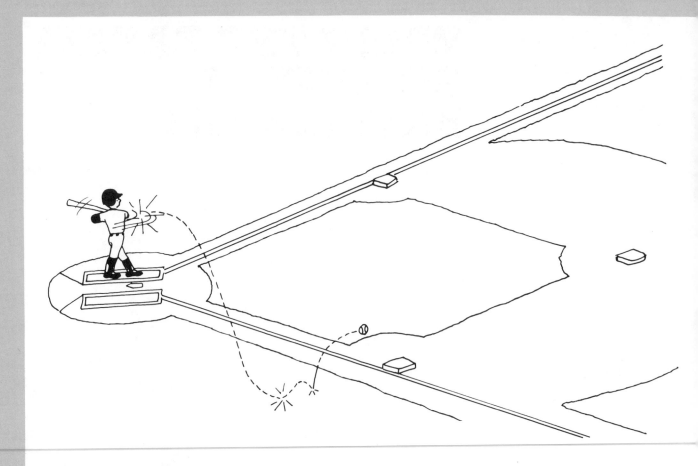

A fair ball is a batted ball that settles on fair ground. A fair fly will be decided by the foul line and not by where the fielder is standing when the ball is touched (rule 2.00).

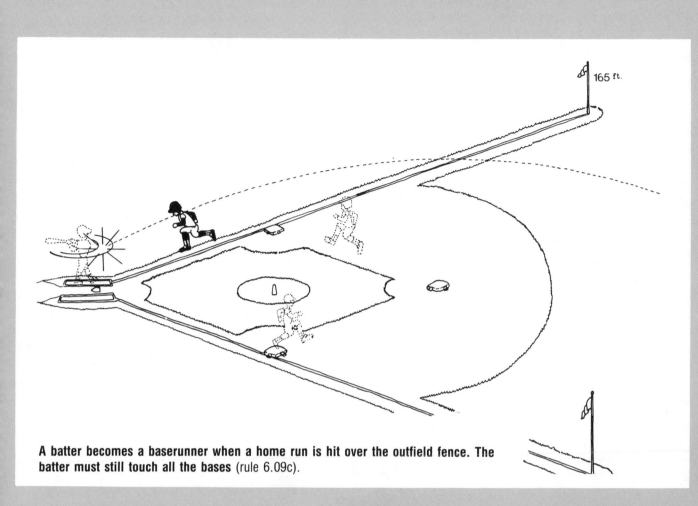

A batter becomes a baserunner when a home run is hit over the outfield fence. The batter must still touch all the bases (rule 6.09c).

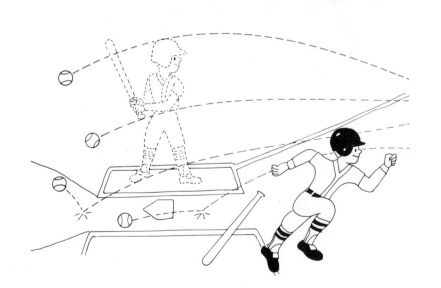

The batter becomes a runner and may walk to first base without danger of being put out if four "balls" have been called by the umpire (rule 6.08a).

A "ball" is a pitch that goes outside the strike zone and that the batter does not try to hit (rule 2.00).

The batter may go to first without being put out if he is touched by a pitch. The batter must have tried to dodge the pitch. A strike will be called if the pitch hits him in the strike zone (rule 6.08).

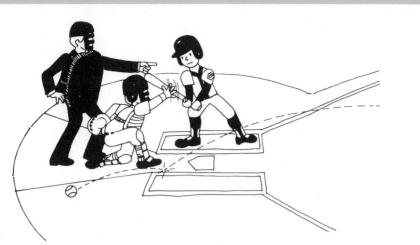

If the catcher or any fielder interferes with the batter, the batter may be given first base without danger of being put out (rule 6.08c).

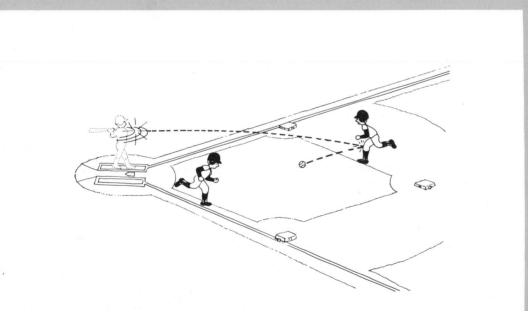

If a fair ball accidentally touches a baserunner before a fielder (other than the pitcher) has had a chance to make a play on it, the batter is given first base (rule 6.08d).

If a fair ball touches an umpire before it is touched by a fielder, the batter will be given first base without being put out (rule 6.08d).

WHEN AND HOW THE RUNNERS MOVE

TO MOVE ALONG THE BASE PATH AND SCORE A RUN, THE RUNNER MUST TOUCH FIRST, SECOND, THIRD, AND HOME BASES, IN THAT ORDER.

If a runner can touch a base before being put out, the runner may stay there safely until forced to move (rule 7.01).

If the pitcher has the ball and he is touching the pitching plate and the catcher is in the catcher's box and ready, the runners may not leave their bases. They may leave when the pitch reaches home plate (rule 7.13).

When a foul ball is not caught, the ball is dead and all runners return, without danger, to their bases (rule 5.09e).

This runner is out. If a fair or foul fly ball is caught, the runners must return to their bases. The runner should return quickly since, if the runner or the base is tagged, he may be called out (rule 7.08).

Two runners cannot be on the same base. If it is not a "force play," the base belongs to the lead runner. The following runner will be out if tagged (rule 7.03).

This is a force play. A force play happens when a runner loses the right to a base because the batter becomes a runner (rule 2.00).

The player on third is not forced. The runner on first is forced.

WHEN A BASERUNNER IS OUT

WHEN A TAG IS LEGALLY MADE BY A FIELDER, BEFORE THE BASERUNNER REACHES BASE SAFELY, THE BASERUNNER IS OUT.

A tag is when a fielder, while holding the ball securely in hand or glove, steps on or touches the base, or touches the runner with the ball (rule 2.00).

First base was tagged before the batter/runner reached it. The runner is out (rule 6.05j).

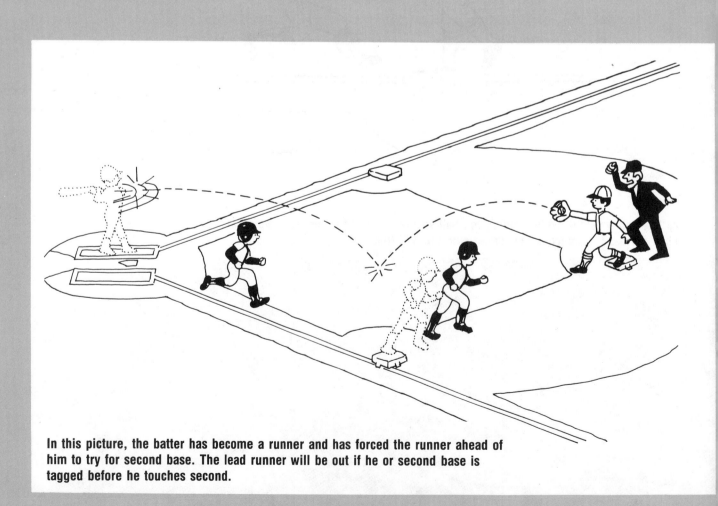

In this picture, the batter has become a runner and has forced the runner ahead of him to try for second base. The lead runner will be out if he or second base is tagged before he touches second.

In this picture, the play is no longer a force play because the batter/runner has been put out. Now, the runner trying for second base must be tagged to be put out (rule 7.08e).

This runner is out. If a fair or foul fly ball is caught, the runners must return to their bases. The runner should return quickly since, if the runner or the base is tagged, he may be called out (rule 7.08d).

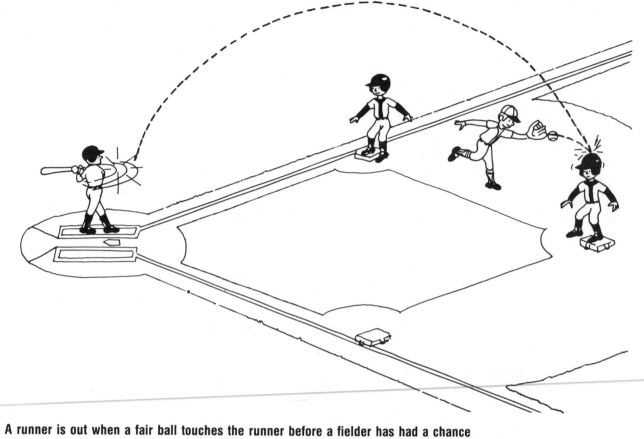

A runner is out when a fair ball touches the runner before a fielder has had a chance to make a play on it. This is true whether the runner is on base or not. The ball is dead and no runners advance (rule 7.08f).

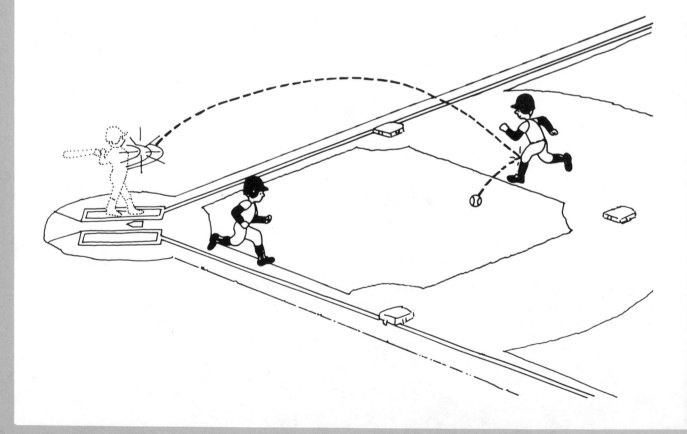

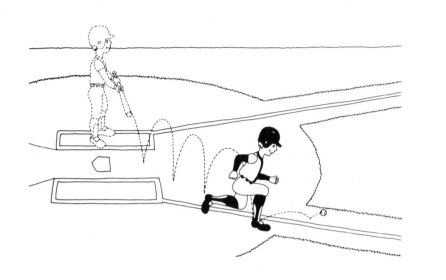

A runner is out if, after hitting or bunting foul, the runner tries to touch the ball and change its path. The ball is then dead (rule 6.05i).

If the runner interferes with a batted ball, a thrown ball, or a fielder on purpose, the runner is out (rule 7.08b).

A baserunner who passes a runner ahead of him who is not out, is out (rule 7.08h).

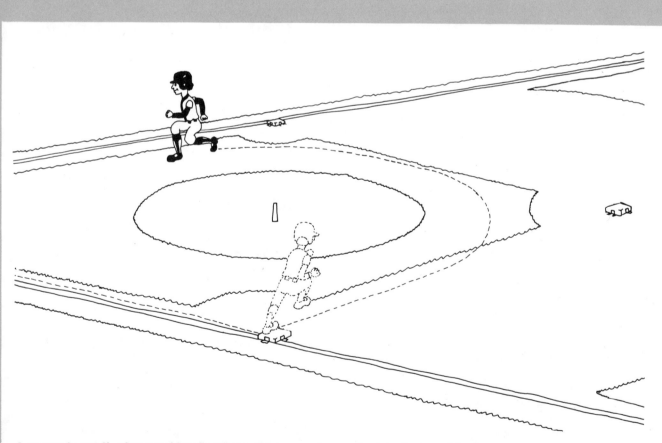

A runner is out if, after touching first base, the runner leaves the baselines and is not even trying to reach the next base (rule 7.08a).

The runner will be out if, to get away from a tag, the runner runs more than three feet away from the line between the bases. Also, the runner may not "ram" a fielder standing near the base path playing the ball (rule 7.08).

If this runner or the base is tagged he can be called out. The manager will have to appeal, which means to point out to the umpire he thinks a base was missed (rule 7.10b).

A runner will be called out on appeal if the runner does not touch home base, makes no attempt to return and touch it, and home base is tagged (rule 7.10d).

A batter/runner cannot be tagged out for touching but overrunning first base. However, to avoid being tagged, the runner must return immediately to first (rule 7.08c).

WHEN ARE BASES "AWARDED" TO RUNNERS?

Each runner, including the batter, may take one base without being put out if a ball is pitched or thrown off the field by the pitcher while the pitcher is standing on the pitching plate (rule 7.05h).

A runner may move to the next base without danger of being put out when the batter's "walk" forces the runner to move (rule 7.04b).

Each runner, including the batter, may advance two bases without danger of being put out when a ball thrown by a fielder goes anywhere off the playing field (rule 7.05g).

Each runner except the batter may take one base without danger of being put out when a fielder, after catching a fly ball, falls into the stands (rule 7.04c).

The ball is dead and the umpire may award the runners as many bases as he thinks they would have reached if a spectator interferes with a live ball (rule 3.16).

What if a fielder interferes with a runner on whom a play is being made? The umpire will award at least one base to the runner, and may award as many bases as he thinks would have been reached if the interference had not happened (rule 7.06a).

If a fielder tries to knock down a fair ball by throwing a glove at it and the glove hits the ball, each runner, including the batter, will be awarded three bases without danger of being put out. If the ball was going for a home run when it was touched, then the ump will award four bases—a homer! (rule 7.05a)

THE PITCHER

The pitcher is the fielder who throws the pitch to the batter.

There are a lot of rules about the pitcher's movements.

A pitcher is allowed eight warm-up pitches at the beginning of each inning (rule 8.03).

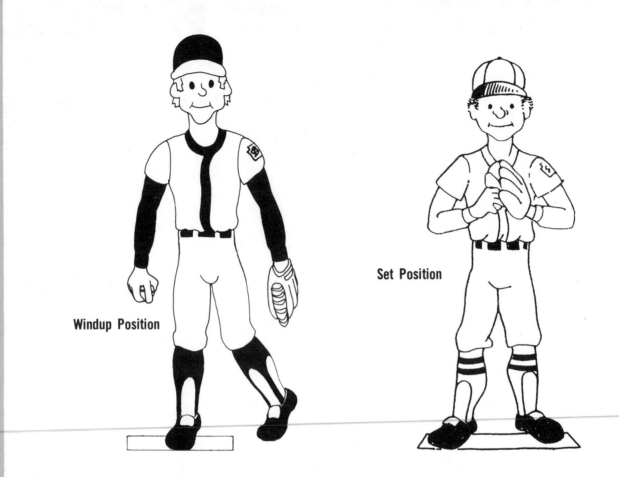

Windup Position

Set Position

There are two legal starting positions for the pitcher, the "windup" position and the "set" position. Either one may be used at any time (rule 8.01).

A pitcher's pivot foot is the foot in contact with the pitcher's plate when the pitch is thrown (rule 2.00).

FRONT (TOWARDS HOME PLATE)

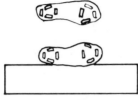
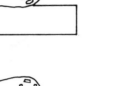
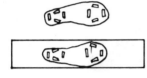
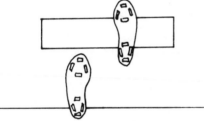
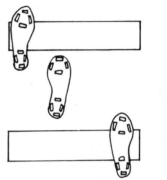

LEGAL

BACK (TOWARDS HOME PLATE)

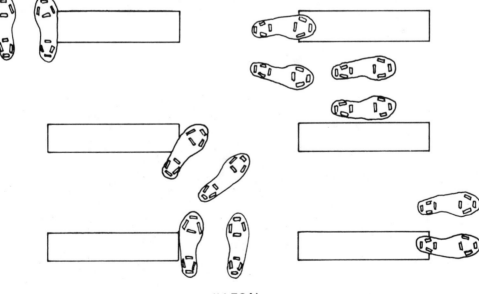

ILLEGAL

Some legal and illegal positions for the pitcher's feet.

Once the pitcher has taken position, the pivot foot shouldn't be lifted from the ground. The other foot may be lifted to take only one step backward and one step forward in the act of pitching the ball (rule 8.01a).

Before taking a set position the pitcher may make any natural motions. This is called the "stretch." The pitcher doesn't need to pause between the stretch and the pitch but must be in the set position at some time in between (rule 8.01b).

A balk is called when the pitcher does something illegal when runners are on base. The penalty for a balk is that the runners may move up one base (rule 2.00).

If there are any runners, a balk will be called if the pitcher—while not touching the pitcher's plate—moves as if he were going to pitch (rule 8.05a).

If there are any runners, it is a balk if the pitcher stands on the pitcher's plate without the ball or while off the pitcher's plate feints a pitch (rule 8.05i).

If there are any runners, a balk will be called when the pitcher drops the ball, even if it is dropped by accident (rule 8.05j).

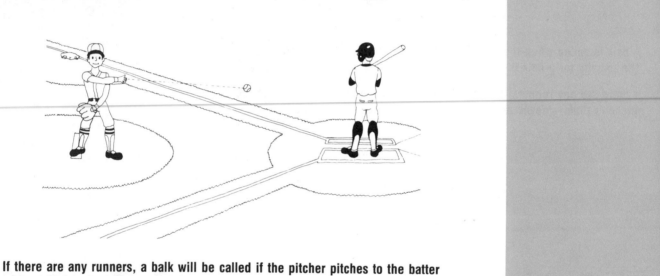

If there are any runners, a balk will be called if the pitcher pitches to the batter without facing the batter (rule 8.05f).

Until the natural pitching motion commits a pitcher to a pitch, he may throw to any base. He must be doing this to catch a runner off base, and must step toward that base as he throws (rule 8.01c).

The pitcher must not *try* to hit the batter when pitching (rule 8.02c).

The pitcher should not pitch a shine ball, spit ball, mud ball, sandpaper ball, ear wax ball, Mighty Bubble bubble gum ball, Veriwhite toothpaste ball, or Dr. Hiram P. MacGullicutty's Baldness Tonic and Liver Potion ball. The pitcher is allowed to rub the ball between bare hands (rule 8.02a-6).

The pitcher should not rub the ball on the glove, clothing, or body (rule 8.02a-4).

The pitcher should not touch the pitching hand to the mouth or lips. Nor should he spit in either hand, in the glove, or on the ball (rule 8.02a-1).

The official scorer keeps many records. One record is of some of the mistakes made by each fielder. They are called errors. These records have no effect on the way the game will be played on the field or who will win (rule 10.02b).

An error is charged for each mistake (missed catch or wild throw) that keeps a runner from being put out or lets the runner take more bases (rule 10.13).

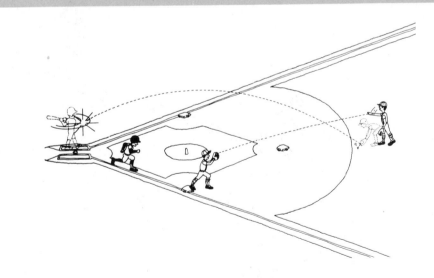

It is not an error if a fielder fumbles a grounder, fly ball or a thrown ball but is then able to control the ball in time to force out a runner at any base (rule 10.14d).

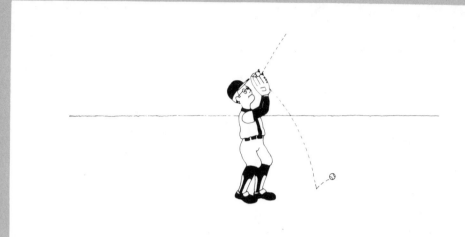

It is an error if a fielder drops a foul fly ball so that a batter gets a longer turn at bat (rule 10.13a).

It is not an error if, before there are two outs, a fielder lets a foul ball land on purpose to keep a runner on third from scoring (rule 10.14e).

It is an error if a runner is able to advance because a fielder does not stop or does not try to stop a well-thrown ball (rule 10.13e).

It is an error if a fielder catches a thrown ball or a ground ball in time to tag first base or the runner but doesn't do so (rule 10.13b).

If a good throw would have put the runner out, it is an error when a fielder's wild throw lets a baserunner reach base safely (rule 10.13d).

It is not an error when a fielder makes a wild throw if the runner would not have been put out even with a good throw (rule 10.14b).

If a fielder's wild throw lets a runner advance, it is an error (rule 10.13d).

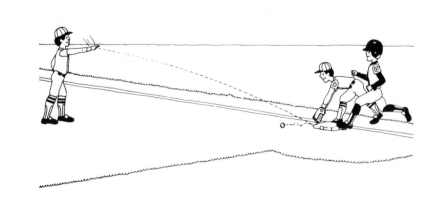

It is an error if a fielder's throw hits a base, umpire, baserunner, etc., and this mistake lets the runner advance (rule 10.13d).

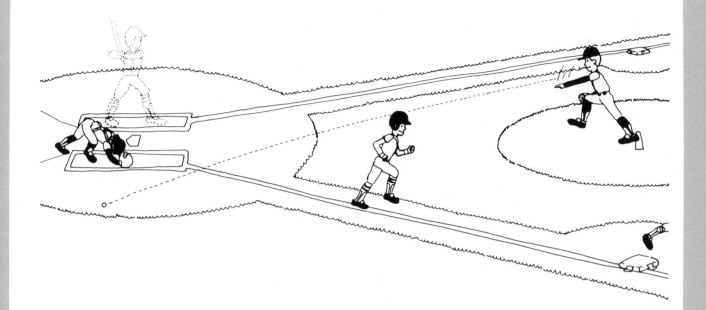

Ball four was a wild pitch and the runner has been given a base on balls. No error is charged if runners advance because of a wild pitch, a passed ball, or a balk (rule 10.14f).

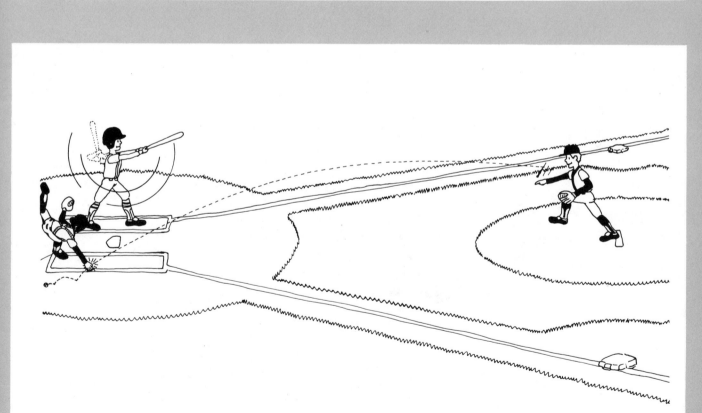

If the third strike is a wild pitch, score a strikeout and a wild pitch (rule 10.14f).

It's not an error if, after a pitch, the catcher makes a wild throw trying to stop someone from stealing. If the wild throw lets the runner advance more bases, though, it *will* be counted as an error (rule 10.14a).

It is not an error if a fielder makes a wild throw while trying to make the second out of a double play; it is an error, however, if the wild throw causes any runners to be able to take more bases than they would have reached if the throw had been good (rule 10.14c).

WHAT'S THE CALL?

A fielder is hit in the glove with a fly ball, but it bounces out, hits against his chest and is trapped, finally, in the crook of the elbow. Is it a catch?
Yes, it's a catch as long as the fielder doesn't later drop it when taking the ball in hand (rule 2.00: Catch).

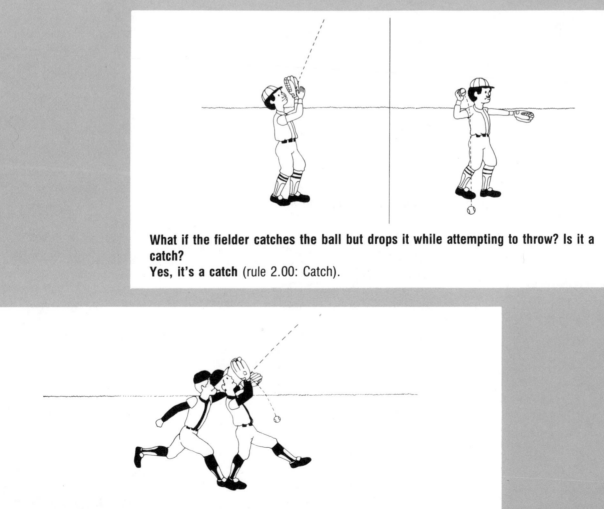

What if the fielder catches the ball but drops it while attempting to throw? Is it a catch?
Yes, it's a catch (rule 2.00: Catch).

An outfielder, while catching the ball, runs into another outfielder and the ball is dropped. Is it a catch?
No, it is not a catch (rule 2.00: Catch).

The ball, fouled straight back from the batter, hits the catcher in the chest and drops into the catcher's glove. Is it a catch? Is the batter out?
No, it's an uncaught foul (rule 2.00: Foul Tip).

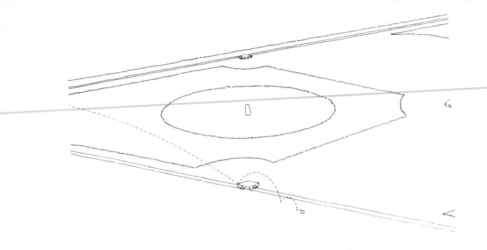

A batted ball hits first base and bounces into foul territory. Fair or foul?
It's fair (rule 2.00: Fair Ball).

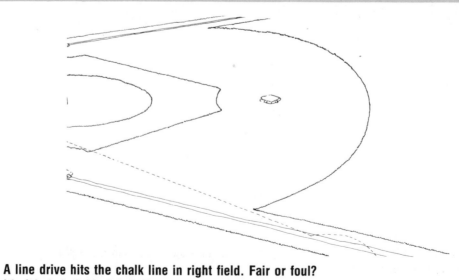

A line drive hits the chalk line in right field. Fair or foul?
It's fair (rule 2.00: Fair Ball).

A runner from third is trapped between home and third by the catcher and third baseman. In the rundown, the baserunner collides with the catcher, who does not have the ball. What's the call?
The runner is awarded the base he was trying to reach (rule 7.06).

If a fielder who does not have possession of the ball or is not fielding the ball tries to keep a runner from reaching a base, it is also Obstruction.

What's the call? A spectator reaches out of the stands and touches a line drive, preventing a fielder from catching it.
The ball is dead and the umpire will decide on whatever penalty he thinks will make things turn out as if the interference never happened (rule 3.16).

The umpire-in-chief stands behind the catcher and is often called the plate umpire (rule 9.04a).

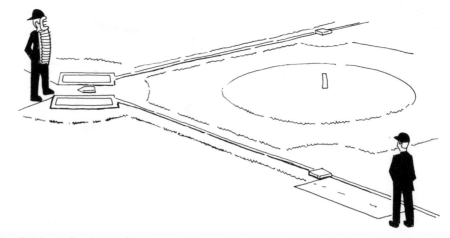

The field umpire may take any position on the field which helps in seeing upcoming plays on the bases (rule 9.04b).

UMPIRE POSITION WHEN THERE IS ONE BASE UMPIRE

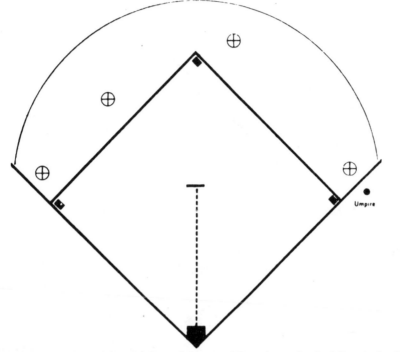

When the bases are empty, the umpire takes a position along the foul line in foul territory just in back of the first baseman.

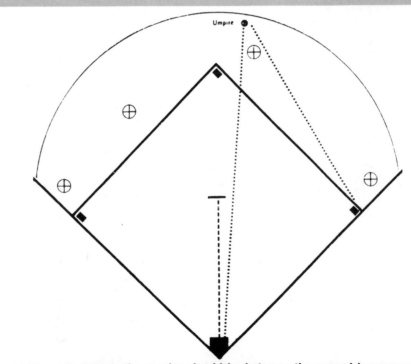

With a runner on first base, the umpire should be between the second baseman and second base. The dotted line shows the line of vision for the umpire. He should be able to see a pitched ball reaching the plate and also keep an eye on the runner at first base.

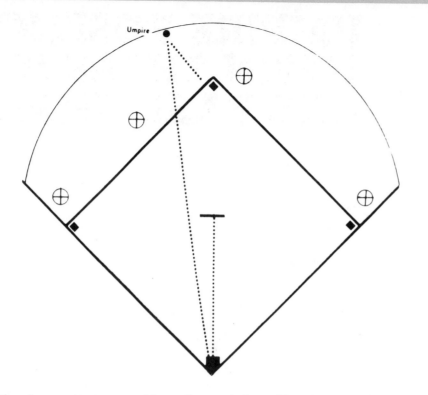

When there's a runner on second base, the umpire's position should be between the shortstop and second base. The line of vision is to the plate and to second base.

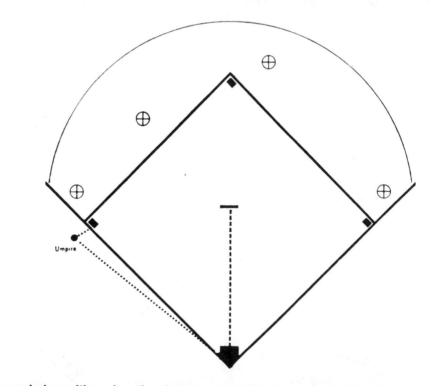

The umpire's position when there's a runner on third base should be in foul territory in back of third base. The dotted line shows the line of vision.

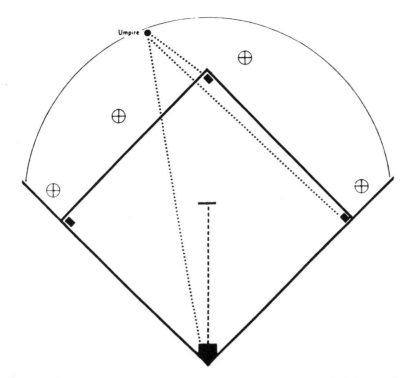

With runners on first and second, it's necessary to maintain a line of vision to the plate, first and second bases. The umpire's position should be between the second baseman and the shortstop.

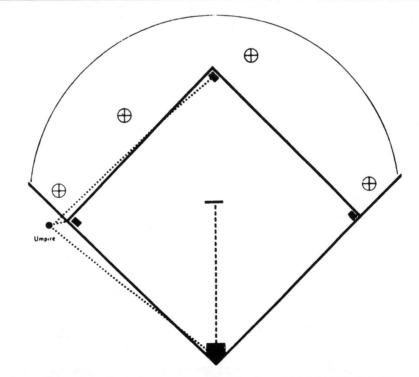

The ump's position when there are runners on second and third is in foul territory just in back of third base. As soon as the ball reaches the batter a quick slight turn of the head to the left will catch a runner on second base.

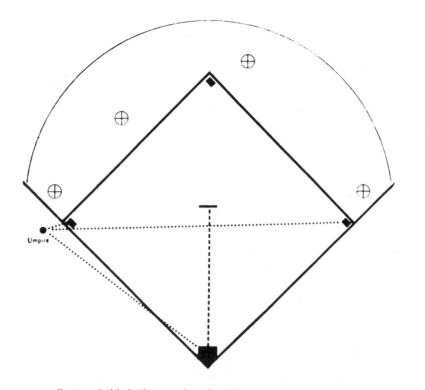

With runners on first and third, the umpire should take a position in foul territory just in back of third base. In this case the umpire has a clear view of the plate, first base and third base areas.

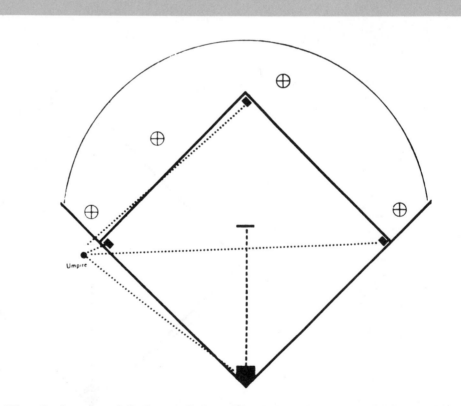

When the bases are full, the umpire's position is in foul territory just back of third base. From here, the umpire can see a pitched ball reach the batter and can also watch runners on first and third bases. As soon as the ball reaches the batter, a quick slight turn of the head to the left will catch the runner on second base.

UMPIRES' SIGNALS

STRIKE
The right arm and hand are moved outward from the body and at least waist high.

SAFE
Both arms are extended in front of the body, palms down. The position should be held long enough to be seen by players, managers and other umpires.

TIME
Arms extended upward, palms out. This position is held until the ump is satisfied that the signal has been seen and observed.

OUT
Right fist is clenched, arm is raised. This signal should be made without hesitation at the instant of the decision.

INTERFERENCE
This is a new signal to clarify "Interference." It applies to both offensive and defensive teams.

LEAVING TOO SOON
The umpire drops a cloth handkerchief or marker. It is the duty of the base umpire to take position to observe the base runner and the pitched ball.

OBSTRUCTION
Usually in such cases the umpire will indicate the base the runner is entitled to or must return to. Hands on the hips indicates obstruction on the part of the defensive team.

BALK
The left arm is extended upward. A balk is usually indicated by a voice signal, but should be accompanied by the hand signal to ensure clarity.

PITCH STRIKES BAT
Both arms are extended upward, slightly in front of the head. Left hand is striking right wrist.

OFFICIAL PLAYING RULES

1.00—OBJECTIVES OF THE GAME

1.01—Little League Baseball is a game between two teams of nine players each, under direction of a manager and coach, played on a regulation Little League field in accordance with these rules, under jurisdiction of one or more umpires.

1.02—The objective of each team is to win by scoring more runs than the opponent.

1.03—The winner of the game shall be that team which shall have scored, in accordance with these rules, the greater number of runs at the conclusion of a regulation game.

1.04—**THE PLAYING FIELD**. The field shall be laid out according to the instructions, supplemented by Diagrams No. 1 and No. 2 on pages 19 and 20.

The infield shall be a 60-foot square.

The outfield shall be the area between two foul lines formed by extending two sides of the square, as in Diagram 1. The distance from home base to the nearest fence, stand or other obstruction on fair territory should be 200 feet or more. A distance of 200 feet or more along the foul lines, and to center field is recommended. The infield shall be graded so that the base line and home plate are level.

The pitcher's plate shall be six inches above the level of home plate. The infield and outfield, including the boundary lines, are fair territory and all other area is foul territory.

It is desirable that the line from home base through the pitcher's plate to second base shall run east-northeast.

It is recommended that the distance from home base to the backstop, and from the base lines to the nearest fence, stand or other obstruction on foul territory should be 25 feet or more. See Diagram 1.

When location of home base is determined, with a steel tape measure 84 feet, 10 inches in desired direction to establish second base. From home base, measure 60 feet towards first base from second base, measure 60 feet towards first base; the intersection of these lines establishes first base. From home base, measure 60 feet towards third base; from second base, measure 60 feet towards third base; the intersection of these lines establishes third base. The distance between first base and third base is 84 feet, 10 inches. All measurements from home base shall be taken from the point where the first and third base lines intersect.

The catcher's box, the batter's boxes, the coaches' boxes, the three-foot first base lines and the next batter's boxes shall be laid out as shown in Diagrams 1 and 2.

The catcher's box extends approximately 6 feet 4¾ inches to the rear of home plate. It is determined by extending each foul line 9 feet beyond the back point of home plate.

The batter's box shall be rectangular, 6 feet by 3 feet. The inside line, if used, shall be parallel to and 4 inches away from the side of home plate. It shall extend forward from the center of home plate 3 feet and to the rear 3 feet.

The coaches' boxes shall be 4 feet by 8 feet and shall not be closer than 6 feet from the foul lines.

The foul lines and all other playing lines indicated in the diagrams by solid black lines shall be marked with chalk or other white material. Caustic lime must not be used.

The grass lines and dimensions shown on the diagrams are those used in many fields, but they are not mandatory. Each league shall determine the size and shape of the grassed and bare areas of its playing field.

1.05—Home base shall be marked by a five-sided slab of whitened rubber. It shall be a 12-inch square with two of the corners filled in so that one edge is 17 inches long, two 8½ inches and two are 12 inches. It shall be set in the ground with the point at the intersection of the lines extending from home base to first base and to third base; with the 17-inch edge facing the pitcher's plate and the two 12-inch edges coinciding with the first and third base lines. The top edges of home base shall be beveled and the base shall be fixed in the ground level with the ground surface. The black beveled edge is not considered part of home plate.

1.06—First, second and third bases shall be marked by white canvas bags, securely attached to the ground. The first and third base bags shall be entirely within the infield. The second base bag shall be centered on second base. The base bags shall be 14 inches square, not more than two and one-fourth (¼) inches thick, and filled with soft material.

NOTE: If the impact of a runner breaks a base loose from its position no play can be made on that runner at that base if the runner had reached the base safely.

1.07—The pitcher's plate shall be a rectangular slab of whitened rubber 18 inches by 4 inches. It shall be set in the ground as shown in Diagrams 1 and 2, so that the distance between the front side of the pitcher's plate and home base (the rear point of home plate) shall be 46 feet.

1.08—The league shall furnish players' benches, one each for the home and visiting teams. Such benches should not be less than twenty-five feet from the base lines. They shall be protected by fencing of wire.

1.09—The ball used must meet Little League specifications and standards. It shall weigh not less than five (5) nor more than five and one-fourth (5¼) ounces, and measure not less than nine (9) nor more than nine and one-fourth (9¼) inches in circumference.

1.10—The bat used must meet Little League specifications and standards. It shall be a smooth, rounded stick and made of wood or of material tested and proved acceptable to Little League standards. It shall not be more than thirty-three (33) inches in length, not more than two and one-quarter (2¼) inches in diameter, and if wood, not less than one and one-sixteenth (1 1/16) inches in diameter (one inch for bats less than 30") at its smallest part. Bats may be taped or fitted with a sleeve for a distance not exceeding sixteen (16) inches from the small end. No laminated bat shall be used. Colored bats are acceptable. An illegal bat must be removed.

1.11—

(a) (1) All players on a team shall wear uniforms identical in color, trim and style. (2) The Official Little League Shoulder Patch must be affixed to the upper left sleeve of the uniform blouse. (3) Any part of an undershirt exposed to view shall be of a uniform solid color (not white) for all players on a team.

(b) A league must provide each team with a distinctive uniform. Uniforms are the property of the league.

(c) (1) Sleeve lengths may vary for individual players, but the sleeves of each individual shall be approximately the same length. (2) No player shall wear ragged, frayed or slit sleeves.

(d) No players shall attach to a uniform tape or other material of a different color than the uniform.

(e) No part of the uniform shall include a pattern that imitates or suggests the shape of a baseball.

(f) Glass buttons and polished metal shall not be used on a uniform.

(g) No player shall attach anything to the heel or toe of the shoe other than toe plate.

(h) Shoes with metal spikes or cleats are not permitted. Shoes with molded cleats are permissible.

(i) Managers and coaches must not wear conventional baseball uniforms or shoes with metal spikes but may wear cap, slacks and shirt.

(j) Players must not wear watches, rings, pins, jewelry or other metallic items.

1.12—The catcher must wear a catcher's mitt (not a first baseman's mitt or fielder's glove) of any shape, size or weight consistent with protecting the hand.

1.13—The first baseman may wear a glove or mitt not more than 12 inches long from top to bottom and not more than eight inches wide across the palm, measured from the base of the thumb crotch to the outer edge of the mitt. The glove may be of any weight.

1.14—Each fielder, other than the first baseman and the catcher may wear a glove not more than 12 inches long nor more than 7¾ inches wide, measured from the base of the thumb crotch to the outer edge of the glove. The glove may be of any weight.

1.15—

(a) The pitcher's glove shall be uniform in color, including all stitching, lacing and webbing. The pitcher's glove may not be white or gray.

(b) No pitcher shall attach to the glove any foreign material of a color different from the glove.

(c) No pitcher shall wear sweat bands on wrists.

1.16—Each league shall provide in the dugout or bench of the offensive team seven (7) protective helmets which must meet Little League specifications and standards. Use of helmet by the batter, on-deck batter, all base runners and coaches is mandatory. Use of helmet by adult base coach is optional. Each helmet shall have an exterior warning label.
NOTE: The warning label cannot be embossed in the helmet, but must be placed on the exterior portion of the helmet and be visible and easy to read.
Effective 1991, the helmets provided by each league must meet NOCSAE specifications and bear the NOCSAE stamp as well as an exterior warning label as noted above.

1.17—All male players must wear athletic supporters. Catchers (male) must wear the metal, fibre or plastic cup type. Catchers must wear long model chest protectors with neck collar, throat guard, shin guards and a catcher's helmet, all of which must meet Little League specifications and standards. Catchers must wear a mask, throat protector and catcher's helmet during practice, pitcher warmup and games.

2.00—DEFINITION OF TERMS

(All definitions in Rule 2.00 are listed alphabetically)

ADJUDGED is a judgement decision by an umpire.

An APPEAL is an act of a fielder in claiming violation of the rules by the offensive team. An appeal must be made verbally.

A BACKSTOP is the barrier erected behind the catcher in order to allow the catcher to retrieve passed balls easily.

A BALK is an illegal act by the pitcher with a runner or runners on base, entitling all runners to advance one base.

A BALL is a pitch which does not enter the strike zone in flight and is not struck at by the batter.

A BASE is one of four points which must be touched by a runner in order to score a run; more usually applied to the canvas bags and the rubber plate which mark the base points.

A BASE COACH is a team member in uniform or one (1) adult manager or coach, who is stationed in the coach's box at first or third base to direct the batter and the runners.

A BASE ON BALLS is an award of first base granted to batters who, during their time at bat receive four pitches outside the strike zone.

A BATTER is an offensive player who takes a position in the batter's box.

BATTER—RUNNER is a term that identifies the offensive player who has just finished a time at bat until that player is put out or until the play on which that player becomes a runner ends.

The BATTER'S BOX is the area within which the batter must stand during a time at bat.

The BATTERY is the pitcher and catcher.

BENCH OR DUGOUT is the seating facilities reserved for players, substitutes, one manager, and one coach when they are not actively engaged on the playing field. Batboys and/or batgirls are not permitted.

A BUNT is a batted ball not swung at, but intentionally met with the bat and tapped slowly.

A CALLED GAME is one in which, for any reason, the umpire-in-chief terminates play.

A CATCH is the act of a fielder in getting secure possession in the hand or glove of a ball in flight and firmly holding it before it touches the ground providing such fielder does not use cap, protector, pocket or any other part of the uniform in getting possession. It is not a catch, however, if simultaneously or immediately following contact with the ball, the fielder collides with a player, or with a wall, or if that fielder falls down, and as a result of such collision or falling, drops the ball. It is not a catch if a fielder touches a fly ball which then hits a member of the offensive team or an umpire and then is caught by another defensive player. If the fielder has made the catch and drops the ball while in the act of making a throw following the catch, the ball shall be adjudged to have been caught. In establishing the validity of the catch, the fielder shall hold the ball long enough to prove complete control of the ball and that release of the ball is voluntary and intentional.

The CATCHER is the fielder who takes the position back of the home base.

The CATCHER'S BOX is that area within which the catcher shall stand until the pitcher delivers the ball.

A COACH is appointed to perform such duties as the manager may designate.

A COACHER is a member of the team roster or an adult coach or manager who occupies the coacher's box at first or third base to direct a base runner or batter.

A DEAD BALL is a ball out of play because of a legally created temporary suspension of play.

The DEFENSE (or DEFENSIVE) is the team, or any player of the team, in the field.

A DOUBLE PLAY is a play by the defense in which two offensive players are put out as a result of continuous action, providing there is no error between putouts.

(a) A force double play is one in which both putouts are force plays.

(b) A reverse force double play is one in which the first out is made at any base and the second out is made by tagging a runner who originally was forced, before the runner touches the base to which that runner was forced.

DUGOUT (see definition of "BENCH")

A FAIR BALL is a batted ball that settles on fair ground between home and first base, or between home and third base, or that is on or over fair territory when bounding to the outfield past first or third base, or that touches first, second or third base, or that first falls on fair territory on or beyond first base or third base, or that, while on or over fair territory touches the person of an umpire or player, or that, while over fair territory, passes out of the playing field in flight.
NOTE: A fair fly shall be adjudged according to the relative position of the ball and the foul line, including the foul pole, and not as to whether the fielder is on fair or foul territory at the time such fielder touches the ball.

FAIR TERRITORY is that part of the playing field within, and including the first base and third base lines, from home base to the bottom of the playing field fence and perpendicularly upwards. Home plate, first base and third base and all foul lines are in fair territory.

A FIELDER is any defensive player.

FIELDER'S CHOICE is the act of a fielder who handles a fair grounder and, instead of throwing it to first base to put out the batter-runner, throws to another base in an attempt to put out a preceding runner. The term is also used by scorers (a) to account for the advance of the batter-runner who takes one or more extra bases when the fielder who handles the safe hit attempts to put out a preceding runner; (b) to account for the advance of a runner (other than by stolen base or error) while a fielder is attempting to put out another runner; and (c) to account for the advance of a runner made solely because of the defensive's team indifference. (Undefended steal).

A FLY BALL is a batted ball that goes high in the air in flight.

A FORCE PLAY is a play in which a runner legally loses the right to occupy a base by reason of the batter becoming a runner.

A FORFEITED GAME is a game declared ended by the umpire-in-chief in favor of the offended team by the score of 6 to 0, for violation of the rules.

A FOUL BALL is a batted ball that settles on foul territory between home and first base, or between home and third base, or that bounds past first or third base on or over foul territory, or that first falls on foul territory beyond first or third base, or that while on or over foul territory, touches the person of an umpire or player, or any object foreign to the natural ground.

NOTE: A foul fly shall be judged according to the relative position of the ball and the foul line, including the foul pole, and not as to whether the fielder is on foul or fair territory at the time that fielder touches the ball.

FOUL TERRITORY is that part of the playing field outside the first and third base lines extended to the fence and perpendicularly upwards.

A FOUL TIP is a batted ball that goes sharp and direct from the bat to the catcher's hands and is legally caught. It is not a foul tip unless caught and any foul tip that is caught is a strike, and the ball is in play. It is not a catch if it is a rebound, unless the ball has first touched the catcher's glove or hand.

A GROUND BALL is a batted ball that rolls or bounces close to the ground.

The HOME TEAM is the team which takes the field first at the start of the game. Adopted schedules will determine which team this will be.

ILLEGAL (or ILLEGALLY) is contrary to these rules.

An ILLEGAL PITCH is (1) a pitch delivered to the batter when the pitcher does not have the pivot foot in contact with the pitcher's plate; (2) when the pitcher delivers the pitch with a foreign substance applied to the ball. Rosin can be applied to the hand; (3) a quick return pitch. Penalty for (1) is a balk. For (2) and (3) check Rule 8.02 (a).

An ILLEGALLY BATTED BALL is one hit by the batter with one or both feet on the ground entirely outside the batter's box.

An INFIELDER is a fielder who occupies a position in the infield.

An INFIELD FLY is a fair fly ball (not including a line drive nor an attempted bunt) which can be caught by an infielder with ordinary effort, when first and second, or first, second and third bases are occupied, before two are out. The pitcher, catcher and any outfielder stationed in the infield on the play shall be considered infielders for the purpose of this rule.

When it seems apparent that a batted ball will be an Infield Fly, the umpire shall immediately declare "Infield Fly" for the benefit of the runners. If the ball is near the baseline, the umpire shall declare "Infield Fly, if Fair."

The ball is alive and runners may advance at the risk of the ball being caught, or retouch and advance after the ball is touched, the same as on any fly ball. If the hit becomes a foul ball, it is treated the same as any foul.

NOTE: If a declared Infield Fly is allowed to fall untouched to the ground, and bounces foul before passing first or third base, it is a foul ball. If a declared Infield Fly falls untouched to the ground, outside the baseline, and bounces fair before passing first or third base, it is an Infield Fly.

IN FLIGHT describes a batted, thrown, or pitched ball which has not yet touched the ground or some object other than a fielder. If the pitch touches the ground and bounces through the strike zone it is a "ball." If such a pitch touches the batter, that batter shall be awarded first base. If the batter hits such a pitch, the ensuing action shall be the same as if the ball was hit in flight.

IN JEOPARDY is a term indicating that the ball is in play and an offensive player may be put out.

An INNING is that portion of a game within which the teams alternate on offense and defense and in which there are three putouts for each team. Each team's time at bat is a half-inning. It will be held that an inning starts the moment the third out is made completing the preceding inning.

INTERFERENCE

(a) Offensive interference is an act by the team at bat which interferes with, obstructs, impedes, hinders or confuses any fielder attempting to make a play. If the umpire declares the batter, batter-runner or a runner out for interference, all other runners shall return to the last base that was, in the judgment of the umpire, legally touched at the time of the interference, unless otherwise provided by these rules.

(b) Defensive interference is an act by a fielder which hinders or prevents a batter from hitting a pitch.

(c) Umpire's interference occurs (1) when an umpire hinders, impedes or prevents a catcher's throw attempting to prevent a stolen base, or (2) when a fair ball touches an umpire on fair territory before passing a fielder.

(d) Spectator interference occurs when a spectator reaches out of the stands or goes on the playing field, and touches a live ball.

(e) On any interference the ball is dead.

The LEAGUE is a group of teams who play each other in a pre-arranged schedule under these rules for the league championship.

LEGAL (or LEGALLY) is in accordance with these rules.

A LINE DRIVE is a batted ball that goes sharp and direct from the bat to a fielder without touching the ground.

A LIVE BALL is a ball which is in play.

The MANAGER is a person appointed by the president to be responsible for the team's actions on the field, and to represent the team in communications with the umpire and the opposing team.

(a) The manager shall always be responsible for the team's conduct, observance of the official rules and deference to the umpires.

(b) If a manager leaves the field, that manager shall designate the coach as a substitute and such substitute manager shall have the duties, rights and responsibilities of the manager.

OBSTRUCTION is the act of a fielder who, while not in possession of the ball or not in the act of fielding the ball, impedes the progress of any runner.

OFFENSE is the team, or any player of the team, at bat.

OFFICIAL RULES. The rules contained in this book.

OFFICIAL SCORER. See Rule 10.00.

An OUT is one of the three required retirements of an offensive team during its time at bat.

An OUTFIELDER is a fielder who occupies a position in the outfield, which is the area of the playing field most distant from home base.

OVERSLIDE (or OVERSLIDING) is the act of an offensive player when the slide to a base, other than when advancing from home to first base, is with such momentum that the player loses contact with the base.

A PENALTY is the application of these rules following an illegal act.

The PERSON of a player or an umpire is any part of the body, clothing or equipment.

A PITCH is a ball delivered to the batter by the pitcher.

A PITCHER is the fielder designated to deliver the pitch to the batter.

The Pitcher's PIVOT FOOT is that foot which is in contact with the pitcher's plate as the pitch is delivered.

"PLAY" is the umpire's order to start the game or to resume action following any dead ball.

A QUICK RETURN is a pitch made with obvious intent to catch a batter off balance. Check Rule 8.02 (a) (7).

REGULATION GAME. See Rules 4.10 and 4.11.

A RETOUCH is the act of a runner returning to a base as legally required.

A RUN (or SCORE) is the score made by an offensive player who advances from batter to runner and touches first, second, third and home bases in that order.

A RUNDOWN is the act of the defense in an attempt to put out a runner between bases.

A RUNNER is an offensive player who is advancing toward, or touching, or returning to any base.

"SAFE" is a declaration by the umpire that a runner is entitled to the base for which that runner was trying.

SET POSITION is one of the two legal pitching positions.

A STRIKE is a legal pitch which meets any of these conditions—

(a) Is struck at by the batter and is missed;

(b) Is not struck at, if any part of the ball passes through any part of the strike zone;

(c) Is fouled by the batter when there is less than two strikes;

(d) Is bunted foul (batter is out and ball is dead, if batter bunts foul on third strike);

(e) Touches the batter's person as the batter strikes at it (dead ball);

(f) Touches the batter in flight in the strike zone; or

(g) Becomes a foul tip (ball is live and in play).

The STRIKE ZONE is that space over home plate which is between the batter's armpits and the top of the knees when the batter assumes a natural stance. The umpire shall determine the strike zone according to the batter's usual stance when that batter swings at a pitch.

A SUSPENDED GAME is a called game which is to be completed at a later date.

A TAG is the action of a fielder in touching a base with the body while holding the ball securely and firmly in the hand or glove; or touching a runner with the ball or with the hand or glove holding the ball, while holding the ball securely and firmly in the hand or glove.

A THROW is the act of propelling the ball with the hand and arm to a given objective and is to be distinguished always from the pitch.

A TIE GAME is a regulation game which is called when each team has the same number of runs.

"TIME" is the announcement by the umpire of a legal interruption of play, during which the ball is dead.

TOUCH. To touch a player or umpire is to touch any part of the player or umpire's body, clothing or equipment.

A TRIPLE PLAY is a play by the defense in which three offensive players are put out as a result of continuous action, providing there is no error between putouts.

A WILD PITCH is one so high, or low, or wide of the plate that it cannot be handled with ordinary effort by the catcher.

WIND-UP POSITION is one of the two legal pitching positions.

3.00—GAME PRELIMINARIES

3.01—Before the game begins the umpires shall—

(a) Require strict observance of all rules governing team personnel, implements of play and equipment of players;

(b) Be sure that all playing lines (heavy lines on Diagrams No. 1 and No. 2) are marked with non-caustic lime, chalk or other white material easily distinguishable from the ground or grass;

(c) Receive from the league a supply of baseballs which meet Little League specifications and standards;

The umpire shall be the sole judge of the fitness of the balls to be used in the game;

(d) Be assured by the league that additional balls are immediately available for use if required;

(e) Have possession of at least two alternate balls and shall require replenishment of such supply of alternate balls as needed throughout the game. Such alternate balls shall be put in play when—

(1) A ball has been batted out of the playing field or into the spectator area;
(2) A ball has become discolored or unfit for further use;
(3) The pitcher requests such alternate ball.

3.02—No player shall intentionally discolor or damage the ball by rubbing it with soil, rosin, paraffin, licorice, sandpaper, emery-paper or other foreign substance.

PENALTY: The umpire shall demand the ball and remove the offender from the game. In case the umpire cannot locate the offender, and if the pitcher delivers such discolored or damaged ball to the batter, the pitcher shall be removed from the game at once.

3.03—A player in the starting line-up who has been removed for a substitute may re-enter the game once, in any position in the batting order, provided:

1. The substitute has completed one time at bat and;
2. Has played defensively for a minimum of six (6) consecutive outs.
3. A pitcher may not re-enter the game as a pitcher.
4. Only a player in the starting line-up may re-enter the game.

NOTE: (1) When two or more substitute players of the defensive team enter the game at the same time, the manager shall, immediately before they take their positions as fielders, designate to the umpire-in-chief such player's positions in the team's batting order and the umpire-in-chief shall notify the official scorer. The umpire-in-chief shall have authority to designate the substitute's places in the batting order, if this information is not immediately provided.

NOTE: (2) Should injury or illness prevent a manager from fielding nine (9) players the manager may, without penalty of forfeiture, replace injured or ill players with a player previously in the line-up—but, only if use of all other eligible players has exhausted the roster. This provision does not apply with respect to a player or players ejected from the game. If a team is unable to field nine (9) players for reasons of ejection of a player and no eligible substitute is available, previously used players may not enter the game.

3.04—A player whose name is on the team's batting order may not become a substitute runner for another member of the team. "Courtesy runner" not permitted.

3.05—

(a) The pitcher named in the batting order handed to the umpire-in-chief, as provided in Rules 4.01 (a) and 4.01 (b) shall pitch to the first batter or any substitute batter until such batter or any substitute batter is put out or reaches first base, unless the pitcher sustains injury or illness which, in the judgment of the umpire-in-chief, incapacitates the pitcher from further play as pitcher.

(b) If the pitcher is replaced, the substitute pitcher shall pitch to the batter then at bat, or any substitute batter, until such batter is put out or reaches first base, or until the offensive team is put out, unless the substitute pitcher sustains injury or illness, which in the umpire-in-chief's judgment, incapacitates the pitcher from further play as a pitcher.

3.06—The manager shall immediately notify the umpire-in-chief of any substitution and shall state to the umpire-in-chief the substitute's place in the batting order.

3.07—The umpire-in-chief, after having been notified, shall immediately announce, or cause to be announced, each substitution.

3.08—

(a) If no announcement of a substitution is made, the substitute shall be considered to have entered the game when—

(1) If a pitcher, the substitute takes position on the pitcher's plate and throws one warmup pitch to the catcher;

(2) If a batter, the substitute takes position in the batters box;
(3) If a fielder, the substitute reaches the position usually occupied by the fielder being replaced and play commences;
(4) If a runner, the substitute takes the place of the runner being replaced.
(b) Any play made by, or on, any of the above mentioned unannounced substitutes shall be legal.

3.09—Players, managers and coaches of the participating teams shall not address, or mingle with spectators, nor sit in the stands during a game in which they are engaged. Managers or coaches must not warm up a pitcher at home plate or in the bull pen at any time. They may, however, stand by to observe a pitcher during warmup in the bull pen.

3.10—
(a) The managers of both teams shall agree on the fitness of the playing field before the game starts. In the event that the two managers cannot agree, the president or a duly delegated representative shall make the determination.

(b) The umpire-in-chief shall be the sole judge as to whether and when play shall be suspended during a game because of unsuitable weather conditions or the unfit condition of the playing field; as to whether and when play shall be resumed after such suspension; and as to whether and when a game shall be terminated after such suspension. Said umpire shall not call the game until at least thirty minutes after play has been suspended. The umpire may continue suspension as long as there is any chance to resume play.

3.11—Double Headers, with the same teams involved, are not permissible under Little League Regulations. (Exception under condition of Rule 4.12)

3.12—When the umpire suspends play, "Time" shall be called. At the umpire's call of "Play" the suspension is lifted and play resumes. Between the call of "Time" and the call of "Play" the ball is dead.

3.13—The local league will establish ground rules to be followed by all teams in the league.

3.14—Members of the offensive team shall carry all gloves and other equipment off the field and to the dugout while their team is at bat. No equipment shall be left lying on the field, either in fair or foul territory.

3.15—No person shall be allowed on the playing field during a game except uniformed players, managers and coaches, umpires and news photographers authorized by the league. In case of intentional interference with play by any person authorized to be on the playing field, the ball is dead at the moment of the interference and no runners on base may advance. Should an overthrown ball accidentally touch an authorized person, it will not be considered interference and the ball will remain live.

3.16—When there is spectator interference with any thrown or batted ball, the ball shall be dead at the moment of interference and the umpire shall impose such penalties as in the umpire's opinion will nullify the act of interference.
APPROVED RULING: If spectator interference clearly prevents a fielder from catching a fly ball, the umpire shall declare the batter out.

3.17—Players and substitutes shall sit on their team's bench or in the dugout unless participating in the game or preparing to enter the game. No one except eligible players in uniform and manager and coach shall occupy the bench or dugout. When batters or base runners are retired, they must return to the bench or dugout at once. Batboys and/or batgirls are not permitted.

3.18—The local league shall provide proper protection sufficient to preserve order and to prevent spectators from entering the field. Either team may refuse to play until the field is cleared.

4.00—STARTING AND ENDING THE GAME

4.01—The umpires shall proceed directly to home plate where they shall be met by the managers of the opposing teams, just preceding the established time to begin the game. In sequence—
(a) The home team manager shall give the batting order in duplicate to the umpire-in-chief;
(b) Next, the visiting manager shall give the batting order in duplicate to the umpire-in-chief;
(c) The umpire-in-chief shall make certain that the original and duplicate copies are the same, then provide a copy of each batting order to the opposing manager. The original copy retained by the umpire shall be the official batting order;
(d) As soon as the home team's batting order is handed to the umpire-in-chief, the umpires are in charge of the playing field and from that moment have sole authority to determine when a game shall be called, halted or resumed on account of weather or the conditions of the playing field.

4.02—The players of the home team shall take their defensive positions, the first batter of the visiting team shall take position in the batter's box, the umpire shall call "Play" and the game shall start.

4.03—When the ball is put in play at the start of, or during a game, all fielders other than the catcher shall be in fair territory.
(a) The catcher shall be stationed directly back of the plate. The catcher may leave that position at any time to catch a pitch or make a play except that when the batter is being given an intentional base on balls, the catcher must stand with both feet within the lines of the catcher's box until the ball leaves the pitcher's hand.
PENALTY: Balk.
(b) The pitcher, while in the act of delivering the ball to the batter, shall take the legal position.
(c) Except the pitcher and the catcher, any fielder may be stationed anywhere in fair territory.
(d) Except the batter, or runner attempting to score, no offensive player shall cross the catcher's lines when the ball is in play.

4.04—The batting order shall be followed throughout the game unless a player is substituted for another. Substitutes must take the place of the replaced player's position in the batting order except as covered by Rule 3.03.

4.05—The offensive team shall station two coachers on the field during its time at bat, one near first base and one near third base. Coachers shall—
(1) Be eligible players in the uniform of their team; or one (1) adult manager or coach.
(2) Remain within the coachers' boxes at all times;
(3) Talk to members of their own team only.
An offending coacher shall be removed from coacher's box.

4.06—No manager, coach or player, shall at any time, whether from the bench or the playing field or elsewhere—
(1) Incite, or try to incite, by word or sign, a demonstration by spectators;
(2) Use language which will in any manner refer to or reflect upon opposing players, an umpire or spectators;
(3) In the umpire's judgment any member of the offensive team makes any move calculated to cause the pitcher to commit a balk.
First warn the player and/or manager. If continued, remove the player and/or manager from the game or bench. If such action causes a balk, it shall be nullified.
(4) No fielder shall take a position in the batter's line of vision, with deliberate intent to distract the batter.
The offender shall be removed from the game.

4.07—When a manager, coach or player is ejected from a game, they shall leave the field immediately and take no further part in that game. They may not sit in the stands and may not be recalled.

4.08—When the occupants of a player's bench show violent disapproval of an umpire's decision, the umpire shall first give warning that such disapproval shall cease. If such action continues—
PENALTY: The umpire shall order the offender out of the game and away from the spectator's area. If the umpire is unable to detect the offender or offenders, the bench may be cleared of all players. The manager of the offending team shall have the privilege of recalling to the playing field only those players needed for substitution in the game.

4.09—HOW A TEAM SCORES
(a) One run shall be scored each time a runner legally advances to and touches first, second, third and home base before three players are put out to end the inning.
EXCEPTIONS: A run is not scored if the runner advances to home base during a play in which the third out is made (1) by the batter-runner before touching first base; (2) by any runner being forced out; or (3) by a preceding runner who is declared out because that runner failed to touch one of the bases (appeal play).
(b) When the winning run is scored in the last half inning of a regulation game, or in the last half of an extra inning, as the result of a base on balls, hit batter or any other play with the bases full which forces the runners to advance, the umpire shall not declare the game ended until runners forced to advance have touched the bases to which they are forced (appeal play).

4.10—
(a) A regulation game consists of six innings, unless extended because of a tie score, or shortened (1) because the home team needs none of its half of the sixth inning or only a fraction of it; or (2) because the umpire calls the game.
(b) If the score is tied after six complete innings, play shall continue until (1) the visiting team has scored more total runs than the home team at the end of a completed inning; or (2) the home team scores the winning run in an uncompleted inning.
(c) If a game is called, it is a regulation game:
(1) If four innings have been completed;
(2) If the home team has scored more runs in three or three and a fraction half innings than the visiting team has scored in four completed half-innings;
(3) If the home team scores one or more runs in its half of the fourth inning to tie the score.
(d) If a game is called before it has become a regulation game, the umpire shall declare it "No Game."
NOTE: For scorekeeping purposes, all batting, fielding and pitching records shall be disregarded. However, the pitcher shall be charged with the number of innings pitched in the current calendar week.

4.11—The score of a regulation game is the total number of runs scored by each team at the moment the game ends.
(a) The game ends when the visiting team completes its half of the sixth inning if the home team is ahead.
(b) The game ends when the sixth inning is completed, if the visiting team is ahead.
(c) If the home team scores the winning run in its half of the sixth inning (or its half of an extra inning after a tie), the game ends immediately when the winning run is scored.
EXCEPTION: If the last batter in a game hits a home run out of the playing field, the batter-runners on base are permitted to score, in accordance with the base-running rules, and the game ends when the batter-runner touches home plate.
APPROVED RULING: The batter hits a home run out of the playing field to win the game in the last half of the sixth or an extra inning, but is called out for passing a preceding runner. The game ends immediately when the winning run is scored.
(d) A called game ends at the moment the umpire terminates play.
EXCEPTION: If the game is called during an uncompleted inning, the game ends at the end of the last previous completed inning in each of the following situations:
(1) The visiting team scores one or more runs to tie the score in the uncompleted inning, and the home team does not score in the uncompleted inning.
(2) The visiting team scores one or more runs to take the lead in the uncompleted inning, and the home team does not tie the score or retake the lead in the uncompleted inning.
(e) A regulation game that is tied after four or more completed innings and halted by the umpire, shall be resumed from the exact point that play was halted. The game shall continue in accordance with Rule 4.10 (a) and 4.10 (b).
NOTE: When TIE game is halted, pitcher of record may continue pitching in the same game on any subsequent date provided said pitcher has observed the required days of rest and has pitching eligibility in the calendar week in which the game is resumed. For scorekeeping purposes, it shall be considered the same game, and all batting, fielding and pitching records will count.

EXAMPLE:

Rule 4.11

	1	2	3	4	5	6
VISITORS	0	0	0	4	1	
HOME	0	0	0	5		

Game called in top of 5th inning on account of rain. Score reverts to last completed inning (4th) and the home team is the winner 5 to 4.

4.12—TIE games halted due to weather, curfew or light failure shall be resumed from the exact point at which they were halted in the original game. It can be completed preceding the next scheduled game between the same teams. A pitcher can pitch in both games on same day subject to the six-inning per week limitation provided in Regulation VI (b). The lineup and batting order of both teams shall be the same as the lineup and batting order at the moment the game was halted, subject to the rules governing substitution. Any player may be replaced by a player who was not in the game prior to halting the original game. No player once removed before the game was halted may be returned to the lineup unless covered by Rule 3.03.

EXAMPLE:

Rule 4.12

Tie games halted due to weather, curfew or light failure shall be resumed from the exact point at which they were halted in the original game.

	1	2	3	4	5	6
VISITORS	0	0	0	0	4	5
HOME	0	0	0	0	4	

Game called in top of 6th inning, visiting team batting with two out, no base runners this is a tie game. Resume the game in the top of the 6th, visiting team at bat, two out.

4.13—DOUBLE HEADERS, See Rule 3.11.
Double Headers cannot be scheduled in Little League Baseball involving the same teams playing in both games. (Exception under condition of Rule 4.12)

4.14—The umpire-in-chief shall order the playing field lights turned on whenever in such umpire's opinion darkness makes further play in daylight hazardous.

4.15—A game may be forfeited to the opposing team when a team—
(1) Being upon the field, refuses to start play within 10 minutes after the appointed hour for beginning the game, unless such delay, in the umpire's judgment, is unavoidable;
(2) Refuses to continue play unless game was terminated by the umpire;
(3) Fails to resume play, after game was halted by the umpire, within one minute after the umpire has called "Play";
(4) Fails to obey within a reasonable time the umpire's order to remove a player from the game;
(5) After warning by the umpire, willfully and persistently violates any rules of the game.
(6) Employs tactics designed to delay or shorten the game.

4.16—If a game cannot be played because of the inability of either team to place nine players on the field before the game begins, this shall not be grounds for automatic forfeiture, but shall be referred to the Board of Directors for a decision.

4.17—A game in progress shall be forfeited to the opposing team when either team is unable or refuses to place nine players on the field (4.16).

4.18—Forfeited games shall be so recorded in the scorebook and the book signed by the umpire-in-chief. A written report stating the reason for the forfeiture shall be sent to the league president within 24 hours, but failure of the umpire to file this report shall not affect the forfeiture.

4.19—PROTESTING GAME
(a) Protest shall be considered only when based on the violation or interpretation of a playing rule or the use of an ineligible player. No protest shall be considered on a decision involving an umpire's judgment. Equipment which does not meet specifications must be removed from the game and shall not be the basis for a protest.
(b) The managers of contesting teams only shall have the right to protest a game (or in their absence, coaches). However, the manager or acting manager may not leave the dugout until receiving permission from an umpire.
(c) Protests shall be made as follows:
 (1) The protesting manager shall immediately, and before any succeeding play begins, notify the umpire that the game is being played under protest.
 (2) Following such notice the umpire shall consult with the associate umpires. If the umpire is convinced that the decision is in conflict with the rules, the umpire shall reverse that decision. If, however, after consultation, the umpire is convinced that the decision is not in conflict with the rules, said umpire shall announce that the game is being played under protest. Failure of the umpire to make such announcement shall not affect the validity of the protest.
(d) Protest made due to use of ineligible player may be considered only if made to the umpire before the final out of the game.
Whenever it is found that an ineligible player is being used, said player shall be removed from the game, and the game shall be continued under protest or not as the protesting manager decides.
(e) Any protest for any reason whatsoever must be submitted by the manager first to the umpire on the field of play and then in writing to the local league president within 24 hours. The umpire-in-chief shall also submit a report immediately.
(f) A committee composed of the president, player agent, league's umpire-in-chief and one or more other officers or directors who are not managers or umpires shall hear and resolve any such protest as above, including playing rules. If protest is allowed, resume game from exact point when infraction occurred.
NOTE 1: This does not pertain to charges of infractions of playing rules or regulations such as field decorum or actions of league personnel or spectators which must be considered and resolved by the Board of Directors.
NOTE 2: All Little League officials are urged to take precautions to prevent protests. When a protest situation is imminent, the potential offenders should be notified immediately. Example: should a manager, official scorer, league official or umpire discover that a pitcher is ineligible at the beginning of the game, or will become ineligible during the game or at the start of the next inning of play, the fact should be brought to the attention of the manager of the team involved. Such action should not be delayed until the infraction has occurred.

5.00—PUTTING THE BALL IN PLAY—LIVE BALL

5.01—At the time set for beginning the game the umpire-in chief shall order the home team to take its defensive positions and the first batter of the visiting team to take position in the batter's box. As soon as all players are in position the umpire-in-chief shall call "Play."

5.02—After the umpire calls "Play" the ball is alive and in play and remains alive and in play until, for legal cause, or at the umpire's call of "Time" suspending play, the ball becomes dead. While the ball is dead, no player may be put out, no bases may be run and no runs may be scored, except that runners may advance one or more bases as the result of acts which occurred while the ball was alive (such as, but not limited to a balk, an overthrow, interference, or a home run or other fair hit out of the playing field).

5.03—The pitcher shall deliver the pitch to the batter who may elect to strike the ball, or who may not offer at it, as such batter chooses.

5.04—The offensive team's objective is to have its batter become a runner, and its runners advance.

5.05—The defensive team's objective is to prevent offensive players from becoming runners, and to prevent their advance around the bases.

5.06—When a batter becomes a runner and touches all bases legally, one run shall be scored for the offensive team.

5.07—When three offensive players are legally put out, that team takes the field and the opposing team becomes the offensive team.

5.08—If a thrown ball accidentally touches a base coach, or a pitched or thrown ball touches an umpire, the ball is alive and in play. However, if the coach interferes with a thrown ball, the runner is out.

5.09—The ball becomes dead and runners advance one base, or return to their bases, without liability to be put out, when—
(a) A pitched ball touches a batter, or the batter's clothing, while in a legal batting position; runners, if forced, advance (see 6.08);
(b) The plate umpire interferes with the catcher's throw attempting to prevent a stolen base; runners return. If catcher's throw gets the runner out, the out stands. No umpire interference;
(c) A balk is committed, runners advance (see Penalty 8.05);
(d) A ball is illegally batted either fair or foul; runners return;
(e) A foul ball not caught, runners return. The umpire shall not put the ball in play until all runners have retouched their bases;
(f) A fair ball touches a runner or an umpire on fair territory before it touches an infielder including the pitcher, or touches an umpire before it has passed an infielder other than the pitcher. Runner hit by fair batted ball is out;
NOTE: If a fair ball goes through, or by an infielder and touches a runner immediately back of said infielder, or touches a runner after being deflected by an infielder, the ball is in play and the umpire shall not declare the runner out. In making such decision, the umpire must be convinced that the ball passed through, or by, the infielder and that no other infielder had the chance to make a play on the ball; runners advance, if forced.
(g) A pitched ball lodges in the catcher's or umpire's mask or paraphernalia; runners advance.

5.10—The ball becomes dead when an umpire calls "Time." Then umpire-in-chief shall call "Time"—
(a) When in said umpire's judgment, weather, darkness or similar conditions make immediate further play impossible;
(b) When light failure makes it difficult or impossible for the umpires to follow the play;
NOTE: A league may adopt its own regulations governing games interrupted by light failure.
(c) When an accident incapacitates a player or an umpire;
 (1) If an accident to a runner is such as to prevent said runner from proceeding to an entitled base, as on a home run hit out of the playing field or an award of one or more bases, a substitute runner shall be permitted to complete the play.
(d) When a manager requests "Time" for a substitution, or for a conference with one of the players;
(e) When the umpire wishes to examine the ball, to consult with either manager, or for any similar cause;
(f) When a fielder, after catching a fly ball, falls into a bench or stand, or falls across ropes into a crowd when spectators are on the field. Runners advance one base, ball is dead;
NOTE: If a fielder, after making a catch, steps into a bench but does not fall, the ball is in play and runners may advance at their own peril.
(g) When an umpire orders a player or any other person removed from the playing field;
(h) Except in the cases stated in paragraphs (b) and (c) (1) of this rule, no umpire shall call "Time" while a play is in progress.

5.11—After the ball is dead, play shall be resumed when the pitcher takes position on the pitcher's plate with a new ball or the same ball in said pitcher's possession and the plate umpire calls "Play." The plate umpire shall call "Play" as soon as the pitcher takes position on the plate with possession of the ball.

6.00—THE BATTER

6.01—
(a) Each player of the offensive team shall bat in the order that their name appears in the team's batting order.
(b) The first batter in each inning after the first inning shall be the player whose name follows that of the last player who legally completed a time at bat in the preceding inning.
NOTE: In the event that while a batter is in the batter's box, the third out of an inning is made on a base runner, the batter then at bat shall be the first batter of the next inning and the count of balls and strikes shall start over.

6.02—
(a) The batter shall take position in the batter's box promptly when it is said batter's time at bat.
(b) The batter shall not leave that position in the batter's box after the pitcher comes to Set Position, or starts a windup.
PENALTY: If the pitcher pitches, the umpire shall call "Ball" or "Strike" as the case may be.
(c) If the batter refuses to take position in the batter's box during a time at bat, the umpire shall order the pitcher to pitch, and shall call "Strike" on each such pitch. The batter may take a proper position after any such pitch, and the regular ball and strike count shall continue, but if the batter does not take proper position before three strikes are called, that batter shall be declared out.

6.03—The batter's legal position shall be both feet within the batter's box.
APPROVED RULING: The lines defining the box are within the batter's box.

6.04—A batter has legally completed a time at bat when put out or becomes a runner.

6.05—A batter is out when—
(a) A fair or foul fly ball (other than a foul tip) is legally caught by a fielder;
(b) A third strike is legally caught by the catcher;
(c) A third strike caught or not caught by the catcher;
(d) Bunting foul on a third strike;
(e) An Infield Fly is declared;
(f) That batter attempts to hit a third strike and is touched by the ball;
(g) A fair ball touches said batter before touching a fielder;
(h) After hitting or bunting a fair ball, while holding the bat, the bat hits the ball a second time in fair territory. The ball is dead and no runner may advance. If the batter-runner drops the bat and the ball rolls against the bat in fair territory and, in the umpire's judgment there was no intention to interfere with the course of the ball, the ball is alive and in play;
(i) After hitting or bunting a foul ball, that runner intentionally deflects the course of the ball in any manner while running to first base. The ball is dead and no runners may advance;
(j) After hitting a fair ball, the batter-runner or first base is tagged before said batter-runner touches first base;
(k) In running the last half of the distance from home base to first base, while the ball is being fielded to first base, the batter-runner runs outside (to the right of) the three-foot line, or inside (to the left of) the foul line, and in the umpire's judgment in so doing interferes with the fielder taking the throw at first base; except that the batter-runner may run outside (to the right of) the three-foot line or inside (to the left of) the foul line to avoid a fielder attempting to field a batted ball;
(l) An infielder intentionally drops a fair fly ball or line drive, with first, first and second, first and third, or first, second and third bases occupied before two are out. The ball is dead and runner or runners shall return to their original base or bases;
APPROVED RULING: In this situation, the batter is not out if the infielder permits the ball to drop untouched to the ground, except when the Infield Fly rule applies.
(m) A preceding runner shall, in the umpire's judgment, intentionally interfere with a fielder who is attempting to catch a thrown ball or to throw a ball in an attempt to complete a play.

6.06—A batter is out for illegal action when—
(a) Hitting an illegally batted ball;
(b) Stepping from one batter's box to the other while the pitcher is in position ready to pitch;
(c) Interfering with the catcher's fielding or throwing by stepping out of the batter's box or making any other movement that hinders the catcher's play at home base.
EXCEPTION: Batter is not out if any runner attempting to advance is put out, or if runner trying to score is called out for batter's interference.

6.07—BATTING OUT OF TURN
(a) A batter shall be called out, on appeal, when failing to bat in proper turn, and another batter completes a time at bat in place of the proper batter. (1) The proper batter may take position in the batter's box at any time before the improper batter becomes a runner or is put out, and any balls and strikes shall be counted in the proper batter's time at bat.
(b) When an improper batter becomes a runner or is put out, and the defensive team appeals to the umpire before the first pitch to the next batter of either team, or before

any play or attempted play, the umpire shall (1) declare the proper batter out; and (2) nullify any advance or score made because of a ball batted by the improper batter or because of the improper batter's advance to first base on a hit, an error, a base on balls, a hit batter or otherwise.

NOTE: If a runner advances, while the improper batter is at bat, on a stolen base, balk, wild pitch or passed ball, such advance is legal.

(c) When an improper batter becomes a runner or is put out, and a pitch is made to the next batter of either team before an appeal is made, the improper batter thereby becomes the proper batter, and the results of such time at bat become legal.

(d) (1) When the proper batter is called out for failing to bat in turn, the next batter shall be the batter whose name follows that of the proper batter thus called out; (2) When an improper batter becomes a proper batter because no appeal is made before the next pitch, the next batter shall be the batter whose name follows that of such legalized improper batter. The instant an improper batter's actions are legalized, the batting order picks up with the name following that of the legalized improper batter.

APPROVED RULINGS

To illustrate various situations arising from batting out of turn, assume a first-inning batting order as follows:

Abel—Baker—Charles—Daniel—Edward—Frank—George—Henry—Irwin.

PLAY (1). Baker bats. With the count 2 balls and 1 strike, (a) the offensive team discovers the error or (b) the defensive team appeals.

RULING: In either case, Abel replaces Baker, with the count 2 balls and 1 strike.

PLAY (2). Baker bats and doubles. The defensive team appeals (a) immediately or (b) after a pitch to Charles.

RULING: Abel is called out and Baker is the proper batter; (b) Baker stays on second and Charles is the proper batter.

PLAY (3). Abel walks. Baker walks. Charles forces Baker. Edward bats in Daniel's turn. While Edward is at bat, Abel scores and Charles goes to second on a wild pitch. Edward grounds out, sending Charles to third. The defensive team appeals (a) immediately or (b) after a pitch to Daniel.

RULING: (a) Abel's run counts and Charles is entitled to second base since these advances were not made because of the improper batter batting a ball or advancing to first base. Charles must return to second base because the advance to third resulted from the improper batter batting a ball. Daniel is called out and Edward is the proper batter; (b) Abel's run counts and Charles stays on third. The proper batter is Frank.

PLAY (4). With the bases full and two out, Henry bats in Frank's turn, and triples, scoring three runs. The defensive team appeals (a) immediately or (b) after a pitch to George.

RULING: (a) Frank is called out and no runs score. George is the proper batter to lead off the second inning; (b) Henry stays on third and three runs score. Irwin is the proper batter.

PLAY (5). After Play (4) (b) above, George continues to bat. (a) Henry is picked off third base for the third out, or (b) George flies out, and no appeal is made. Who is the proper leadoff batter in the second inning.

RULING: (a) Irwin became the proper batter as soon as the first pitch to George legalized Henry's triple; (b) Henry. When no appeal was made, the first pitch to the leadoff batter of the opposing team legalized George's time at bat.

PLAY (6). Daniel walks and Abel comes to bat. Daniel was an improper batter and if an appeal is made before the first pitch to Abel, Abel is out, Daniel is removed from base, and Baker is proper batter. There is no appeal and a pitch is made to Abel. Daniel's walk is now legalized, and Edward thereby becomes the proper batter. Edward can replace Abel at any time before Abel is put out, or becomes a runner. Edward does not do so. Abel flies out, and Baker comes to bat. Abel was an improper batter, and if an appeal is made before the first pitch to Baker, Edward is out, and the proper batter is Frank. There is no appeal, and a pitch is made to Baker. Abel's out is now legalized, and the proper batter is Baker. Baker walks. Charles is the proper batter. Charles flies out. Now Daniel is the proper batter, but Daniel is on second base. Who is the proper batter?

RULING: The proper batter is Edward. When the proper batter is on base, that batter is passed over, and the following batter becomes the proper batter.

6.08—The batter becomes a runner and is entitled to first base without liability to be put out (provided said runner advances to and touches first base) when—

(a) Four "balls" have been called by the umpire;

(b) The batter is touched by a pitched ball which the batter is not attempting to hit unless (1) The ball is in the strike zone when it touches the batter, or (2) The batter makes no attempt to avoid being touched by the ball;
NOTE: If the ball is in the strike zone when it touches the batter, it shall be called a strike, whether or not the batter tries to avoid the ball. If the ball is outside the strike zone when it touches the batter, it shall be called a ball if that batter makes no attempt to avoid being touched.
APPROVED RULING: When the batter is touched by a pitched ball which does not entitle that batter to first base, the ball is dead and no runner may advance.

(c) The catcher or any fielder interferes with the batter. If a play follows the interference, the manager of the offense may advise the plate umpire of a decision to decline the interference penalty and accept the play. Such election shall be made immediately at the end of the play. However, if the batter reaches first base on a hit, an error, a base on balls, a hit batsman, or otherwise, and all other runners advance at least one base, the play proceeds without reference to the interference;

(d) A fair ball touches an umpire or a runner on fair territory before touching a fielder.
NOTE: If a fair ball touches an umpire after having passed a fielder other than the pitcher, or having touched a fielder, including the pitcher, the ball is in play.

6.09—The batter becomes a runner when—

(a) A fair ball is hit;

(b) A fair ball, after having passed a fielder other than the pitcher, or after having been touched by a fielder, including the pitcher, shall touch an umpire or runner on fair territory;

(c) A fair fly ball passes over a fence or into the stands at a distance from home base of 165 feet or more. Such hit entitles the batter to a home run when all bases have been legally touched. A fair fly ball that passes out of the playing field at a point less than 165 feet from home base shall entitle the batter to advance to second base only;

(d) A fair ball, after touching the ground, bounds into the stands, or passes through, over or under a fence, or through or under a scoreboard, or through or under shrubbery, or vines on the fence, in which case the batter and runners shall be entitled to advance two bases;

(e) Any fair ball which, either before or after touching the ground, passes through or under a fence, or through or under a scoreboard, or through any opening in the fence or scoreboard, or through or under shrubbery or vines on the fence or which sticks in a fence or scoreboard in which case the batter and the runners shall be entitled to two bases;

(f) Any bounding fair ball is deflected by the fielder into the stands, or over or under a fence on fair or foul territory, in which case the batter and all runners shall be entitled to advance two bases;

(g) Any fair fly ball is deflected by the fielder into the stands, or over the fence into foul territory, in which case the batter shall be entitled to advance to second base; but if deflected into the stands or over the fence in fair territory, the batter shall be entitled to a home run. However, should such a fair fly be deflected at a point less than 165 feet from home plate, the batter shall be entitled to two bases only.
NOTE: If deflection occurs off fielder's glove below the fence that batter shall be entitled to two bases.

7.00—THE RUNNER

7.01—A runner acquires the right to an unoccupied base when that runner touches it before being put out. The runner is then entitled to it until put out or forced to vacate it for another runner legally entitled to that base.

7.02—In advancing, a runner shall touch first, second, third and home base in order. If forced to return, the runner shall retouch all bases in reverse order, unless the ball is dead under any provision of Rule 5.09. In such cases, the runner may go directly to the original base.

7.03—Two runners may not occupy a base, but if, while the ball is alive, two runners are touching the base, the following runner shall be out when tagged. The preceding runner is entitled to the base.

7.04—Each runner, other than the batter, may, without liability to be put out, advance one base when—

(a) There is a balk;

(b) The batter's advance without liability to be put out forces the runner to vacate a base, or when the batter hits a fair ball that touches another runner or the umpire before such ball has been touched by, or has passed a fielder, if the runner is forced to advance;

(c) A fielder, after catching a fly ball, falls into a bench or stand, or falls across ropes into a crowd when spectators are on the field;
NOTE: When a runner is entitled to a base without liability to be put out, while the ball is in play, or under any rule in which the ball is in play after the runner reaches an entitled base, and the runner fails to touch the base to which that runner is entitled before attempting to advance to the next base, the runner shall forfeit the exemption from liability to be put out and may be put out by tagging the base or by tagging the runner before that runner returns to the missed base.

7.05—Each runner including the batter-runner may, without liability to be put out, advance—

(a) To home base scoring a run, if a fair ball goes out of the playing field in flight and the runner touches all bases legally; or if a fair ball which, in the umpire's judgment, would have gone out of the playing field in flight (165 feet from home plate), is deflected by the act of a fielder in throwing a glove, cap, or any article of apparel;

(b) Three bases, if a fielder deliberately touches a fair ball with a cap, mask or any part of that fielder's uniform detached from its proper place on the person of said fielder. The ball is in play and the batter may advance to home plate at the batter's peril;

(c) Three bases, if a fielder deliberately throws a glove and touches a fair ball. The ball is in play and batter may advance to home plate at that batter's own peril;

(d) Two bases, if a fielder deliberately touches a thrown ball with a cap, mask or any part of the uniform detached from its proper place on the person of said fielder. The ball is in play;

(e) Two bases, if a fielder deliberately throws a glove at and touches a thrown ball. The ball is in play;

(f) Two bases, if a fair ball bounces or is deflected into the stands outside the first or third base foul line; or if it goes through or under a field fence, or through or under a scoreboard, or through or under shrubbery or vines on the fence; or if it sticks in such fence, scoreboard, shrubbery or vines;

(g) Two bases when, with no spectators on the playing field, a thrown ball goes into the stands, or into a bench (whether or not the ball rebounds into the field), or over or under or through a field fence, or on a slanting part of the screen above the backstop, or remains in the meshes of wire screen protecting spectators. The ball is dead. When such wild throw is the first play by an infielder, the umpire, in awarding such bases, shall be governed by the position of the runners at the time the ball was pitched; in all other cases the umpire shall be governed by the position of the runners at the time the wild throw was made;

APPROVED RULING: If all runners, including the batter-runner have advanced at least one base when infielder makes a wild throw on the first play after the pitch, the award shall be governed by the position of the runners when the wild throw was made.

(h) One base, if a ball, pitched to the batter, or thrown by the pitcher from the position on the pitcher's plate to a base to catch a rummer goes into a stand or a bench, or over or through a field fence or backstop. The ball is dead;

(i) One base, if the batter becomes a runner on a ball four when the pitch passes the catcher and lodges in the umpire's mask or paraphernalia.
NOTE: If the batter becomes a runner on a wild pitch which entitles the runners to advance one base, the batter-runner shall be entitled to first base only.

7.06—When the obstruction occurs, the umpire shall call or signal "Obstruction."

(a) If a play is being made on the obstructed runner, or if the batter-runner is obstructed before touching first base, the ball is dead and all runners shall advance without liability to be put out, to the bases they would have reached, in the umpire's judgment, if there had been no obstruction. The obstructed runner shall be awarded at least one base beyond the base last legally touched by such runner, before the obstruction. Any preceding runners forced to advance by the award of bases as the penalty for obstruction shall advance without liability to be put out;

(b) If no play is being made on the obstructed runner, the play shall proceed until no further action is possible. The umpire shall then call "Time" and impose such penalties, if any as in that umpire's judgment will nullify the act of obstruction.

7.08—Any runner is out when—

(a) (1)Running more than three feet away from a direct line between bases to avoid being tagged, unless such action is to avoid interferences with a fielder fielding a batted ball; or (2) after touching first base the runner leave the baseline, obviously abandoning all effort to touch the next base; or (3) the runner does not slide or attempt to get around a fielder who has the ball and is waiting to make the tag;

(b) Intentionally interferes with a thrown ball; or hinders a fielder attempting to make a play on a batted ball;

(c) That runner is tagged, when the ball is alive, while off a base;
EXCEPTION: A batter-runner cannot be tagged out after overrunning or oversliding first base if said batter-runner returns immediately to the base.
APPROVED RULING: (1) If the impact of a runner breaks a base loose from its position, no play can be made on that runner at that base if the runner had reached the base safely.
APPROVED RULING: (2) If a base is dislodged from its position during a play, any following runner on the same play shall be considered as touching of occupying the base if, in the umpire's judgment, that runner touches or occupies the point marked by the disoldged bag.

(d) Falling to retouch the base after a fair or foul fly ball is legally caught before that runner or the base is tagged by a fielder. The runner shall not be called out for failure to retouch the base after the first following pitch, or any play or attempted play. This is an appeal play;

(e) Failing to reach the next base before a fielder tags said runner or the base after that runner has been forced to advance by reason of the batter becoming a runner. However, if a following runner is put out on a force play, the force is removed and the runner must be tagged to be put out. The force is removed as soon as the runner touches the base to which that runner is forced to advance, and if oversliding or overrunning the base, the runner must be tagged to be put out. However, if the forced runner, after touching the next base, retreats for any reason towards the base last occupied, the force play is reinstated and the runner can again be put out if the defense tags the base to which the runner is forces;

(f) Touched by a fair ball territory before the ball has touched or passed an infielder. The ball is dead and no runner may score, no runners advance, except runners forced to advance;

EXCEPTION: If a runner is touching a base when touched by an Infield Fly, that runner is not out, although the batter is out.
NOTE: If a runner is touched by an Infield Fly when not touching a base, both runner and batter are out.

(g) Attempting to score on a play in which the batter interferes with the play at home base before two are out. With two out, the interference puts the batter out and no score counts;

(h) Passes a preceding runner before such runner is out;

(i) After acquiring legal possession of a base, the runner runs the bases in reverse order for the purpose of confusing the defense or making a travesty of the game. The umpire shall immediately call "Time" and declare the runner out;

(j) Failing to return at once to first base after overrunning or oversliding that base. If attempting to run to second the runner is out when tagged. If after overrunning or oversliding first base, the runner starts toward the dugout, or toward a position, and fails to return to first base at once, that runner is out on appeal, when said runner or the base is tagged;

(k) In running or sliding for home base, the runner fails to touch home base and makes no attempt to return to the base, when a fielder holds the ball in hand, while touching home base, and appeals to the umpire for the decision.

7.09—It is interference by a batter or a runner when —

(a) After a third strike the batter hinders the catcher in an attempt to field the ball;

(b) After hitting or bunting a fair ball, while holding the bat, the bat of such batter hits the ball a second time in fair territory. The ball is dead and no runners may advance. If the batter-runner drops the bat and the ball rolls against the bat in fair territory and, in the umpire's judgment, there was no intention to interfere with the course of the ball, the ball is alive and in play;

(c) The batter intentionally deflects the course of a foul ball in any manner;

(d) Before two are out and a runner on third base, the batter hinders a fielder in making a play at home base; the runner is out;

(e) Any member or members of the offensive team stand or gather around any base to which a runner is advancing, to confuse, hinder or add to the difficulty of the fielders. Such runner shall be declared out for the interference of teammate or teammates;

(f) Any batter or runner who has just been put out hinders or impedes any following play being made on a runner. Such runner shall be declared out for the interference of a teammate;

(g) If, in the judgment of the umpire, a base runner willfully and deliberately interferes with a batted ball or a fielder in the act of fielding a batted ball with the obvious intent to break up a double play, the ball is dead. The umpire shall call the runner out for interference and also call out the batter-runner because of the action of the runner. In no event may bases be run or runs scored because of such action by a runner;

(h) If, in the judgment of the umpire, a batter-runner willfully and deliberately interferes with a batted ball or a fielder in the act of fielding a batted ball, with the obvious intent to break up a double play, the ball is dead; the umpire shall call the batter-runner out for interference and shall also call out the runner who advanced closest to the home plate regardless where the double play might have been possible. In no event shall bases be run because of such interference;

(i) In the judgment of the umpire, the base coach at third base, or first base, by touching or holding the runner, physically assists that runner in returning to or leaving third base or first base;

(j) With a runner on third base, the base coach leaves the box and acts in any manner to draw a throw by a fielder;

(k) In running the last half of the distance from home base to first base while the ball is being fielded to first base, the batter-runner runs outside (to the right of) the three-foot line, or inside (to the left of) the foul line and, in the umpire's judgment, interferes with the fielder taking the throw at first base or attempting to field a batted ball;

(l) The runner fails to avoid a fielder who is attempting to field a batted ball, or intentionally interferes with a thrown ball, provided that if two or more fielders attempt to field a batted ball, and the runner comes in contact with one or more of them, the umpire shall determine which fielder is entitled to the benefit of this rule, and shall not declare the runner out for coming in contact with a fielder other than the one the umpire determines to be entitled to field such a ball;

(m) A fair ball touches the batter or runner in fair territory before touching a fielder. If a fair ball goes through or by an infielder and touches a runner immediately back of said infielder or touches the runner after having been deflected by a fielder, the umpire shall not declare the runner out for being touched by a batted ball. In making such decision, the umpire must be convinced that the ball passed through or by the infielder and that no other infielder had the chance to make a play on the ball, if in the judgment of the umpire, the runner deliberately and intentionally kicks such a batted ball on which the infielder had missed a play, then the runner shall be called out for interference.
PENALTY FOR INTERFERENCE: The runner is out and the ball is dead.

7.10—Any runner shall be called out on appeal —

(a) After a fly ball is caught the runner fails to retouch the base before said runner or the base is tagged;

(b) With the ball in play, while advancing or returning to a base, the runner fails to touch each base in order before said runner, or a missed base, is tagged;
APPROVED RULING: (1) No runner may return to touch a missed base after a following runner has scored. (2) When the ball is dead no runner may return to touch a missed base or one abandoned after said runner has advanced to and touched a base beyond the missed base.

(c) The runner overruns or overslides first base and fails to return to the base immediately, and said runner or the base is tagged;

(d) The runner fails to touch home base and makes no attempt to return to that base, and home base is tagged.

Any appeal under this rule must be made before the next pitch, or any play or attempted play. If the violation occurs during a play which ends a half-inning, the appeal must be made before the defensive team leaves the field. (The defensive team has left the field when no players remain in fair territory.)

An appeal is not to be interpreted as a play or an attempted play.

Successive appeals may not be made on a runner at the same base. If the defensive team on its first appeal errs, a request for a second appeal on the same runner at the same base shall not be allowed by the umpire. (Intended meaning of the word "err" is that the defensive team in making an appeal threw the ball out of play. For example, if the pitcher threw to first base to appeal and threw the ball into the stands, no second appeal would be allowed).

NOTE: Appeal plays may require an umpire to recognize an apparent "fourth out." If the third out is made during a play in which an appeal play is sustained on another runner, the appeal play decision takes precedence in determining the out. If there is more than one appeal during a play that ends a half-inning, the defense may elect to take the out that gives it the advantage. For the purposes of this rule, the defensive team has "left the field" when all players have left fair territory on their way to the bench or dugout.

7.11—The players, coaches or any member of an offensive team shall vacate any space (including both dugouts) needed by a fielder who is attempting to field a batted or thrown ball.

PENALTY: Interference shall be called and the batter or runner on whom the play is being made shall be declared out.

7.12—Unless two are out, the status of a following runner is not affected by a preceding runner's failure to touch or retouch a base. If, upon appeal, the preceding runner is the third out, no runners following the preceding runner shall score. If such third out is the result of a force play, neither preceding nor following runners shall score.

7.13—When a pitcher is in contact with the pitcher's plate and in possession of the ball and the catcher is in the catcher's box ready to receive delivery of ball, base runners shall not leave their bases until the ball has been delivered and has reached the batter.

The violation by one base runner shall affect all other base runners —

(a) When a base runner leaves the base before the pitched ball has reached the batter and the batter does not hit the ball, the runner is permitted to continue. If a play is made on the runner and the runner is out, the out stands. If said runner reaches safely the base to which the runner is advancing, that runner must be returned to the base occupied before the pitch was made, and no out results;

(b) When a base runner leaves the base before the pitched ball has reached the batter and the batter hits the ball, the base runner or runners are permitted to continue. If a play is made and the runner or runners are put out, the out or outs will stand. If not put out, the runner or runners must return to the original base or bases or to the unoccupied base nearest the one that was left;

In no event shall the batter advance beyond first base on a single or error, second base on a double or third base on a triple. The umpire-in-chief shall determine the base value of the hit ball.

(c) When any base runner leaves the base before the pitched ball has reached the batter and the batter bunts or hits a ball within the infield no run shall be allowed to score. If three runners were on the bases and the batter reaches first base safely, each runner shall advance to the base beyond the one they occupied at the start of the play except the runner who occupied third base, which runner shall be removed from the base without a run being scored.
NOTE: See exceptions following this rule.
EXCEPTION: If at the conclusion of the play there is an open base, paragraphs (a) and (b) will apply.

EXAMPLES:

1. Runner on first leaves too soon, batter reaches first safely, runner goes to second.
2. Runner on second leaves too soon, batter reaches first safely, runner returns to second.
3. Runner on third leaves too soon, batter reaches first safely, runner returns to third.
4. Runner on first leaves too soon, batter hits clean double, runner goes to third only.
5. Runner on second leaves too soon, batter hits clean double, runner goes to third only.
6. Runner on third leaves too soon, batter hits clean double, runner returns to third.
7. All runners on base will be allowed to score when the batter hits a clean triple or home run, regardless of whether any runner left too soon.
8. Runners on first and second, either leaves too soon, batter reaches first safely, runners go to second and third.
9. Runners on first and second, either leaves too soon, batter hits clean double, runner on first goes to third, runner on second scores.
10. Runners on first and third, either leaves too soon, batter reaches first safely, runner on first goes to second, runner on third remains there.
11. Runners on first and third, either leaves too soon, batter hits a clean double, runner on first goes to third, runner on third scores.
12. Runners on second and third, either leaves too soon, batter reaches first safely neither runner can advance.
13. Runners on second and third, either leaves too soon, batter hits a clean double, runner on third scores, runner on second goes to third.
14. Runners on first, second and third, any runner leaves too soon, batter hits clean double, runners on second, third score, runner on first goes to third.
15. Bases full, any runner leaves too soon, batter reaches first safely on any ball bunted or hit within the infield, all runners advance one base except runner advancing from third. Runner advancing from third is removed, no run is scored and no out charged. If on the play, a putout at any base results in an open base, runner who occupied third base returns to third base.
16. Bases full, any runner leaves too soon, batter received a base on balls or is hit by a pitch each runner will advance one base and a run will score.

NOTE: When an umpire detects a base runner leaving the base too soon, that umpire shall drop a signal flag or handkerchief immediately to indicate the violation.
NOTE: For purpose of these examples, it is assumed that the batter-runner remains at the base last acquired safely.

8.00—THE PITCHER

8.01—Legal pitching delivery. There are two legal pitching positions, the Windup Position and the Set Position, and either position may be used at any time.

Pitchers shall take signs from the catcher while standing on the rubber.

(a) The Windup Position. The pitcher shall stand facing the batter, the entire pivot foot on, or in front of and touching and not off the end of the pitcher's plate, and the other foot free. From this position any natural movement associated with the delivery of the ball to the batter commits the pitcher to pitch without interruption or alteration. The pitcher shall not raise either foot from the ground, except that in the actual delivery of the ball to the batter, said pitcher may take one step backward, and one step forward with the free foot.
NOTE: When a pitcher holds the ball with both hands in front of the body, with the entire pivot foot on, or in front of and touching but not off the end of the pitcher's plate, and the other foot free, that pitcher will be considered in a Windup Position.

(b) The Set Position. Set Position shall be indicated by the pitcher when that pitcher stands facing the batter with the entire pivot foot on, or in front of, and in contact with, and not off the end of the pitcher's plate, and the other foot in front of the pitcher's plate, holding the ball in both hands in front of the body. From such Set Position the pitcher may deliver the ball to the batter, throw to a base or step backward off the pitcher's plate with the pivot foot. Before assuming Set Position, the pitcher may elect to make any natural preliminary motion such as that known as "the stretch." But if the pitcher so elects, that pitcher shall come to Set Position before delivering the ball to that batter.
NOTE: The pitcher need not come to a complete stop. See Rule 7.13.

(c) At any time during the pitcher's preliminary movements and until the natural pitching motion commits that pitcher to the pitch, said pitcher may throw to any base provided the pitcher steps directly toward such base before making the throw.

(d) If the pitcher makes an illegal pitch with the bases unoccupied, it shall be called a ball unless the batter reaches first base on a hit, an error, a base on balls, a hit batter or otherwise.

(e) If the pitcher removes the pivot foot from contact with the pitcher's plate by stepping backward with that foot, that pitcher thereby becomes an infielder and in the case of a wild throw from that position, it shall be considered the same as a wild throw by any other infielder.

8.02—The pitcher shall not —

(a) (1) Bring the pitching hand in contact with the mouth or lips while in the 10 ft. circle surrounding the pitching rubber;
PENALTY: For violation of this part of the rule the umpires shall immediately

call a ball and warn the pitcher that repeated violation of any part of this rule can cause the pitcher to be removed from the game. However, if the pitch is made and a batter reaches first base on a hit, an error, a hit batsman or otherwise, and no other runner is put out before advancing at least one base, the play shall proceed without reference to the violation.

(2) Apply a foreign substance of any kind to the ball;

(3) Expectorate on the ball, either hand or the glove;

(4) Rub the ball on the glove, person or clothing;

(5) Deface the ball in any manner;

(6) Deliver what is called the "shine" ball, "spit" ball, "mud" ball or "emery" ball. The pitcher, of course is allowed to rub off the ball between the bare hands;

(7) Deliver a "quick" return pitch.

PENALTY: For violation of any part of this rule 8.02 (a), (2 thru 7) umpire shall: Call pitch a ball and warn pitcher.

If play occurs on violation, manager of the offense may advise the plate umpire of acceptance of the play. (Such election must be made immediately at end of play.)

(b) Intentionally delay the game by throwing the ball to players other than the catcher, when the batter is in position, except in an attempt to retire a runner;

PENALTY: If, after warning by the umpire, such delaying action is repeated, the pitcher can be removed from the game.

(c) Intentionally pitch at the batter. If, in the umpire's judgment, such violation occurs, the umpire shall warn the pitcher and the manager of the defense that another such pitch will mean immediate expulsion of the pitcher. If such pitch is repeated during the game, the umpire shall eject the pitcher from the game.

8.03—When a pitcher takes position at the beginning of each inning, that pitcher shall be permitted to pitch not to exceed eight preparatory pitches to the catcher during which play shall be suspended. Such preparatory pitches shall not consume more than one minute of time. If a sudden emergency causes a pitcher to be summoned into the game without any opportunity to warm up, the umpire-in-chief shall allow the pitcher as many pitches as the umpire deems necessary.

8.04—When the bases are unoccupied, the pitcher shall deliver the ball to the batter within 20 seconds after the pitcher receives the ball. Each time the pitcher delays the game by violating this rule, the umpire shall call "Ball."

NOTE: The intent of this rule is to avoid unnecessary delays. The umpire shall insist that the catcher return the ball promptly to the pitcher, and that the pitcher take position on the rubber promptly.

8.05—If there is a runner, or runners, a balk occurs when —

(a) The pitcher, while touching the plate, makes any motion naturally associated with the pitch and fails to make such delivery;

(b) The pitcher, while touching the plate, feints a throw to first base and fails to complete the throw;

(c) The pitcher while touching the plate, fails to step directly toward a base before throwing to that base;

(d) The pitcher while touching the plate, throws, or feints a throw to an unoccupied base, except for the purpose of making a play;

(e) The pitcher makes an illegal pitch;

(f) The pitcher delivers the ball to the batter while not facing the batter;

(g) The pitcher makes any motion naturally associated with the pitch while not touching the pitcher's plate;

(h) The pitcher unnecessarily delays the game;

(i) The pitcher, without having the ball, stands on or astride the pitcher's plate or while off the plate feints a pitch;

(j) The pitcher, while touching the plate, accidentally or intentionally drops the ball;

(k) The pitcher, while giving an intentional base on balls, pitches when the catcher is not in the catcher's box.

PENALTY: The ball is dead, and each runner shall advance one base without liability to be put out, unless the batter reaches first on a hit, an error, a base on balls, a hit batter, or otherwise, and all other runners advance at least one base in which case the play proceeds without reference to the balk. When balk is called if pitch is delivered it will be considered neither a ball nor strike unless the pitch is ball four (4) awarding the batter first base and forcing all runners on base to advance.

APPROVED RULING: In cases where a pitcher balks and throws wild, either to a base or to home plate, a runner or runners may advance beyond the base to which they are entitled at their own risk.

APPROVED RULING: A runner who misses the first base to which that runner is advancing and who is called out on appeal shall be considered as having advanced one base for the purpose of this rule.

8.06—The following rule governs the visit of the manager or coach to the pitcher at the foul line:

(a) This rule limits the number of visits a manager or coach may make to any one pitcher in any one inning;

(b) A third trip to the same pitcher in the same inning will cause this pitcher's automatic removal;

(c) The manager or coach is prohibited from making a third visit while the same batter is at bat.

A manager or coach may not confer with any other defensive player. The catcher may be included in visit with pitcher.

9.00—THE UMPIRE

9.01—

(a) The league president shall appoint one or more umpires to officiate at each league game. The umpire shall be responsible for the conduct of the game in accordance with these official rules and for maintaining discipline and order on the playing field during the game.

NOTE: Plate umpire must wear mask, shin guards and chest protector. Male umpire must wear protective cup.

(b) Each umpire is the representative of the league and of Little League Baseball, and is authorized and required to enforce all of these rules. Each umpire has authority to order a player, coach, manager or league officer to do or refrain from doing anything which affects the administering of these rules and to enforce the prescribed penalties.

(c) Each umpire has authority to rule on any point not specifically covered in these rules.

(d) Each umpire has authority to disqualify any player, coach, manager or substitute for objecting to decisions or for unsportsmanlike conduct or language and to eject such disqualified person from the playing field. If an umpire disqualifies a player while a play is in progress, the disqualification shall not take effect until no further action is possible in that play.

(e) All umpires have authority at their discretion to eject from the playing field (1) any person whose duties permit that person's presence on the field, such as ground crew members, photographers, newsmen, broadcasting crew members, etc. and (2) any spectator or other person not authorized to be on the playing field.

9.02—

(a) Any umpire's decision which involves judgment, such as, but not limited to, whether a batted ball is fair or foul, whether a pitch is a strike or a ball, or whether a runner is safe or out, is final. No player, manager, coach or substitute shall object to any such judgment decisions.

(b) If there is reasonable doubt that any umpire's decision may be in conflict with the rules, the manager may appeal the decision and ask that a correct ruling be made. Such appeal shall be made only to the umpire who made the protested decision.

(c) If a decision is appealed, the umpire making the decision, may ask another umpire for information before making a final decision. No umpire shall criticize, seek to reverse or interfere with another umpire's decision unless asked to do so by the umpire making it.

(d) No umpire may be replaced during a game unless injured or ill.

9.03—

(a) If there is only one umpire, that umpire shall have complete jurisdiction in administering the rules. This umpire may take any position on the playing field which will enable said umpire to discharge all duties (usually behind the catcher, but sometimes behind the pitcher if there are runners).

(b) If there are two or more umpires, one shall be designated umpire-in-chief and the others field umpires.

9.04—

(a) The umpire-in-chief shall stand behind the catcher. This umpire usually is called the plate umpire. The umpire-in-chief's duties shall be to:

(1) Take full charge of, and be responsible for, the proper conduct of the game;

(2) Call and count balls and strikes;

(3) Call and declare fair balls and fouls except those commonly called by field umpires;

(4) Make all decisions on the batter;

(5) Make all decisions except those commonly reserved for the field umpires;

(6) Decide when a game shall be forfeited;

(7) Inform the official scorer of the official batting order; and any changes in the lineups and batting order, on request;

(8) Announce any special ground rules.

(b) A field umpire may take any position (see Little League Umpire Manual) on the playing field best suited to make impending decisions on the bases. A field umpire's duties shall be to:

(1) Make all decisions on the bases except those specifically reserved to the umpire-in-chief;

(2) Take concurrent jurisdiction with the umpire-in-chief in calling "Time," balks, illegal pitches, or defacement or discoloration of the ball by any player;

(3) Aid the umpire-in-chief in every manner in enforcing the rules, and excepting the power to forfeit the game, shall have equal authority with the umpire-in-chief in administering and enforcing the rules and maintaining discipline.

(c) If different decisions should be made on one play by different umpires, the umpire-in-chief shall call all the umpires into consultation, with no manager or player present. After consultation, the umpire-in-chief (unless another umpire may have been designated by the league president) shall determine which decision shall prevail, based on which umpire was in best position and which decision was most likely correct. Play shall proceed as if only the final decision had been made.

9.05—

(a) The umpire shall report to the league president within twenty-four hours after the end of a game all violations of rules and other incidents worthy of comment, including the disqualification of any manager, coach or player, and the reasons therefore.

(b) When any manager, coach or player is disqualified for a flagrant offense such as the use of obscene or indecent language, or an assault upon an umpire, manager, coach or player, the umpire shall forward full particulars to the league president within twenty-four hours after the end of the game.

(c) After receiving the umpire's report that a manager, coach or player has been disqualified, the league president shall require such manager, coach or player to appear before at least three members of the Board of Directors to explain his conduct. In the case of a player, the manager shall appear with the player in the capacity of an advisor. The members of the Board present at the meeting shall impose such penalty as they feel is justified.

9.06—Umpires shall not wear shoes with metal spikes or cleats.

IMPORTANT

Carry your Rule Book. It is better to consult the Rules and hold up the game long enough to decide a knotty problem than to have a game protested and possibly replayed.

10.00—THE OFFICIAL SCORER

INDEX

Assists, 10.11
Base hits, 10.05, 10.06, 10.07
Bases on Balls, 10.16
Box scores, 10.02, 10.03
Caught stealing, 10.08
Determine value of hits, 10.07
Earned runs, 10.18
Errors, 10.13, 10.14
Official scorer, 10.01
Passed balls, 10.15
Percentages, how determined, 10.21
Putouts, 10.10
Runs, batted in, 10.04
Sacrifices, 10.09
Saves for relief pitchers, 10.20
Stolen bases, 10.08
Strikeouts, 10.17
Wild pitches, 10.15
Winning-losing pitcher, 10.19

10.01—

(a) The league president shall appoint an official scorer for each league. The scorer shall have sole authority to make all decisions involving judgment, such as whether a batter's advance to first base is the result of a hit or an error. The scorer shall communicate such decisions to the press by hand signals or over the loudspeaker system and shall advise the announcer of such decisions if requested. In the event of a question of eligibility of a pitcher the record of the Official Scorer shall be deemed official.

(b) (1) To achieve uniformity in keeping the records, the scorer shall conform strictly to the Scoring Rules. The scorer shall have authority to rule on any point not specifically covered in these rules.

(2) If the teams change sides before three are put out, the scorer shall immediately inform the umpire of the mistake.

(3) If the game is protested or play suspended, the scorer shall make note of the exact situation at the time of the protest or suspension, including the score, the number of outs, the position of any runners, and the ball and strike count on the batter.

(4) The scorer shall not make any decision conflicting with the Official Playing rules, or with an umpire's decision.

(5) The scorer shall not call the attention of the umpire or of any member of either team to the fact that a player is batting out of turn.

(c) The scorer is an official representative of the league, and is entitled to the respect and dignity of the office.

10.02—The official score report shall make provisions for entering the information listed below, in a form convenient for the compilation of permanent statistical records:

(a) The following records for each batter and runner:

(1) Number of times they batted, except that no time at bat shall be charged against a player when

(i) The player hits a sacrifice bunt or sacrifice fly

(ii) The player is awarded first base on four called balls

(iii) The player is hit by a pitched ball

(iv) The player is awarded first base because of interference or obstruction

(2) Number of runs scored
(3) Number of safe hits
(4) Number of runs batted in
(5) Two-base hits
(6) Three-base hits
(7) Home runs
(8) Total bases on safe hits
(9) Stolen bases
(10) Sacrifice bunts
(11) Sacrifice flies
(12) Total number of bases on balls
(13) Separate listing of any intentional bases on balls
(14) Number of times hit by a pitched ball
(15) Number of times awarded first base for interference or obstruction
(16) Strikeouts

(b) The following records for each fielder:
(1) Number of putouts
(2) Number of assists
(3) Number of errors
(4) Number of double plays participated in
(5) Number of triple plays participated in

(c) The following records for each pitcher:
(1) Number of innings pitched
NOTE: In computing innings pitched, count each putout as one-third of an inning. If a starting pitcher is replaced with one out in an inning, credit that pitcher 1/3 inning.
If a relief pitcher retires two batters and is replaced, credit that pitcher with 2/3 inning pitched.
(2) Total number of batters faced
(3) Number of batters officially at bat against pitcher, computed according to 10.02 (a) (1)
(4) Number of hits allowed
(5) Number of runs allowed
(6) Number of earned runs allowed
(7) Number of home runs allowed
(8) Number of sacrifice hits allowed
(9) Number of sacrifice flies allowed
(10) Total number of bases on balls allowed
(11) Separate listing of any intentional bases on balls allowed
(12) Number of batters hit by pitched balls
(13) Number of strikeouts
(14) Number of wild pitches
(15) Number of balks

(d) The following additional data:
(1) Name of the winning pitcher
(2) Name of the losing pitcher
(3) Names of the starting pitcher and the finishing pitcher for each team

(e) Number of passed balls allowed by each catcher.

(f) Names of players participating in double plays and triple plays.
EXAMPLE: (1) Double Plays — Jones, Roberts and Smith
(2) Triple Plays — Jones and Smith

(g) Number of runners left on base by each team. This total shall include all runners who get on base by any means and who do not score and are not put out. Include in this total a batter-runner whose batted ball results in another runner being retired for the third out.

(h) Names of batters who hit home runs with bases full.

(i) Names of batters who ground into force double plays and reverse force double plays.

(j) Names of runners caught stealing.

(k) Number of outs when winning run scored, if game is won in last half-inning.

(l) The score by innings for each team.

(m) Names of umpires, listed in this order (1) plate umpire, (2) first base umpire, (3) second base umpire, (4) third base umpire.

(n) Time required to play the game, with delays for weather or light failure deducted.

10.03—
(a) The official scorer shall list each player's name and fielding position or positions in the order in which the player batted, or would have batted if the game ends before the player gets to bat.
NOTE: When a player does not exchange positions with another fielder but is merely placed in a different spot for a particular batter, do not list this as a new position.

(b) Any player who enters the game as a substitute batter or substitute runner, whether or not continuing in the game thereafter, shall be identified in the batting order by a special symbol which shall refer to a separate record of substitute batters and runners. Lower case letters are recommended as symbols for substitute batters, and numerals for substitute runners. The record of substitute batters shall describe what the substitute batter did.
EXAMPLES: "a-Singled for ________ in third inning; b-Flied out for ________ in sixth inning; c-Forced ________ for ________ in seventh inning; d-Grounded out for ________ in ninth inning; 1-Ran for ________ in ninth inning."

HOW TO PROVE A BOX SCORE

(c) A box score is in balance (or proved) when the total of the team's time at bat, bases on balls received, hit batters, sacrifice bunts, sacrifice flies and batters awarded first base because of interference or obstruction, equals the total of that team's runs, players left on base and the opposing team's putouts.

(d) When a player bats out of turn, and is put out, and the proper batter is called out before the ball is pitched to the next batter, charge the proper batter with a time at bat and score the putout and any assists the same as if the correct batting order had been followed. If an improper batter becomes a runner and the proper batter is called out for having missed a turn at bat, charge the proper batter with a time at bat, credit the put out to the catcher and ignore everything entering into the improper batter's safe arrival on base. If more than one batter bats out of turn in succession score all plays just as they occur, skipping the turn at bat of the player or players who first missed batting in the proper order.

CALLED AND FORFEITED GAMES

(e) (1) If a regulation game is called, include the record of all individual and team actions up to the moment the game ends, as defined in Rules 4.10 and 4.11. If it is a tie game, do not enter a winning or losing pitcher.
(2) If a regulation game is forfeited, include the record of all individual and team actions up to the time of forfeit. If the winning team by forfeit is ahead at the time of forfeit, enter as winning and losing pitchers the players who would have qualified if the game had been called at the time of forfeit. If the winning team by forfeit is behind or if the score is tied at the time of forfeit, do not enter in winning or losing pitcher. If a game is forfeited before it becomes a regulation game, include no records. Report only the fact of the forfeit.

RUNS BATTED IN

10.04—
(a) Credit the batter with a run batted in for every run which reaches home base because of the batter's safe hit, a sacrifice bunt, sacrifice fly, infield out or fielder's choice; or which is forced over the plate by reason of the batter becoming a runner with the bases full (on a base on balls, or an award of first base for being touched by a pitched ball, or for interference or obstruction).
(1) Credit a run batted in for the run scored by the batter who hits a home run. Credit a run batted in for each runner who is on base when the home run is hit and who scores ahead of the batter who hits the home run.
(2) Credit a run batted in for the run scored when, before two are out, an error is made on a play on which a runner from third base ordinarily would score.

(b) Do not credit a run batted in when the batter grounds into a force double play or a reverse double play.

(c) Do not credit a run batted in when a fielder is charged with an error because of muffing a throw at first base which would have completed a force double play.

(d) Scorer's judgment must determine whether a run batted in shall be credited for a run which scores when a fielder holds the ball, or throws to a wrong base. Ordinarily, if the runner keeps going, credit a run batted in; if the runner stops and takes off again when noticing the misplay, credit the run as scored on a fielder's choice.

BASE HITS

10.05—A base hit shall be scored in the following cases:

(a) When a batter reaches first base (or any succeeding base) safely on a fair ball which settles on the ground or touches a fence before being touched by a fielder, or which clears a fence;

(b) When a batter reaches first base safely on a fair ball hit with such force, or so slowly that any fielder attempting to make a play with it has no opportunity to do so;
NOTE: A hit shall be scored if the fielder attempting to handle the ball cannot make a play, even if such fielder deflects the ball from or cuts off another fielder who could have put out a runner.

(c) When a batter reaches first base safely on a fair ball which takes an unnatural bounce so that a fielder cannot handle it with ordinary effort, or which touches the pitcher's plate or any base (including home plate) before being touched by a fielder and bounces so that a fielder cannot handle it with ordinary effort;

(d) When a batter reaches first base safely on a fair ball which has not been touched by a fielder and which is in fair territory when it reaches the outfield unless in the scorer's judgment it could have been handled with ordinary effort;

(e) When a fair ball which has not been touched by a fielder touches a runner or an umpire;
EXCEPTION: Do not score a hit when a runner is called out for having been touched by an Infield Fly.

(f) When a fielder unsuccessfully attempts to put out a preceding runner, and in scorer's judgment the batter-runner would not have been put out at first base by ordinary effort.
NOTE: In applying the above rules, always give the batter the benefit of the doubt. A safe course to follow is to score a hit when exceptionally good fielding of a ball fails to result in a putout.

10.06—A base hit shall not be scored in the following cases:

(a) When a runner is forced out by a batted ball, or would have been forced out except for a fielding error;

(b) When a batter apparently hits safely and a runner who is forced to advance by reason of the batter becoming a runner fails to touch the first base to which that runner is advancing and is called out on appeal. Charge the batter with a time at bat but no hit;

(c) When the pitcher, the catcher or any infielder handles a batted ball and puts out a preceding runner who is attempting to advance one base or return to an original base, or would have put out such runner with ordinary effort except for a fielding error. Charge the batter with a time at bat but no hit;

(d) When a fielder fails in an attempt to put out a preceding runner, and in the scorer's judgment the batter-runner could have been put out at first base;
NOTE: This shall not apply if the fielder merely looks toward or feints toward another base before attempting to make the putout at first base.

(e) When a runner is called out for interference with a fielder attempting to field a batted ball, unless in the scorer's judgment the batter-runner would have been safe had the interference not occurred.

DETERMINING VALUE OF BASE HITS

10.07—Whether a safe hit shall be scored as a one-base hit, two-base hit, three-base hit or home run when no error or putout results shall be determined as follows:

(a) Subject to the provisions of 10.07 (b) and (c), it is a one-base hit if the batter stops at first base; it is a two-base hit if the batter stops at second base; it is a three-base hit if the batter stops at third base; it is a home run if the batter touches all bases and scores.

(b) When, with one or more runners on base, the batter advances more than one base on a safe hit and the defensive team makes an attempt to put out a preceding runner, the scorer shall determine whether the batter made a legitimate two-base hit or three-base hit, or whether the batter advanced beyond first base on the fielder's choice.
NOTE: Do not credit the batter with a three-base hit when a preceding runner is put out at the plate, or would have been out but for an error. Do not credit the batter with a two-base hit when a preceding runner trying to advance from first base is put out at third base, or would have been put out but for an error. However, with the exception of the above, do not determine the value of base hits by the number of bases advanced by the preceding runner. A batter may deserve a two-base hit even though a preceding runner advanced one or no bases; a batter may deserve only a one-base hit even though the batter reaches second base and a preceding runner advanced two bases.
EXAMPLES: (1) Runner on first, batter hits to right fielder, who throws to third base in an unsuccessful attempt to put out runner. Batter takes second base. Credit batter with one-base hit. (2) Runner on second. Batter hits fair fly ball. Runner holds up to determine if ball is caught and advances only to third base, while batter takes second. Credit batter with two-base hit. (3) Runner on third. Batter hits high fair fly. Runner takes lead, then runs back to tag up, thinking ball will be caught. Ball falls safe, but runner cannot score, although batter has reached second. Credit batter with two-base hit.

(c) When the batter attempts to make a two-base hit or a three-base hit by sliding, that batter must hold the last base to which said batter advances. If the batter overslides and is tagged out before getting back to the base safely, that batter shall be credited with as many bases as were attained safely. If that batter overslides second base and is tagged out, that batter shall be credited with a one-base hit; if the batter overslides third base, and is tagged out, that batter shall be credited with a two-base hit.
NOTE: If the batter overruns second or third base and is tagged out trying to return, that batter shall be credited with the last base touched. If the batter runs past second after reaching that base standing, attempts to return and is tagged out, said batter shall be credited with a two-base hit. If the batter runs past third base after reaching that base standing, attempts to return and is tagged out, said batter shall be credited with a three-base hit.

(d) When the batter, after making a safe hit, is called out for having failed to touch a base, the last base reached safely shall determine if that batter shall be credited with a one-base hit, a two-base hit or a three-base hit. If the batter is called out after missing home base, that batter shall be credited with a three-base hit. If the batter is called out for missing third base, that batter shall be credited with a two-base hit. If the batter is called out for missing second base, that batter shall be credited with a one-base hit. If the batter is called out for missing first base, that batter shall be charged with a time at bat, but no hit.

(e) When the batter-runner is awarded two bases, three bases or a home run under the provisions of Playing Rules 7.05 or 7.06 (a), that batter-runner shall be credited with a two-base hit, a three-base hit or a home run, as the case may be.

GAME-ENDING HITS

(f) Subject to the provisions of 10.07 (g), when the batter ends a game with a safe hit which drives in as many runs as are necessary to put the team in the lead, the batter shall be credited with only as many bases on the hit as are advanced by the runner who scores the winning run, and then only if the batter runs out the hit for as many bases as are advanced by the runner who scores the winning run.
NOTE: Apply this rule even when the batter is theoretically entitled to more bases because of being awarded an "automatic" extra base hit under various provisions of Playing Rules 6.09 and 7.05.

(g) When the batter ends a game with a home run hit out of the playing field, that batter and any runners on base are entitled to score.

STOLEN BASES

10.08—A stolen base shall be credited to a runner who advances one base unaided by a hit, a putout, an error, a force-out, a fielder's choice, a passed ball, a wild pitch or a balk, subject to the following:

(a) When a runner starts for the next base after the ball reaches the batter and the pitch results in what ordinarily is scored a wild pitch or passed ball, credit the runner with a stolen base and do not charge the misplay.
EXCEPTION: If, as a result of the misplay, the stealing runner advances an extra base, or another runner also advances, score the wild pitch or passed ball as well as the stolen base.

(b) When a runner is attempting to steal, and the catcher, after receiving the pitch, makes a wild throw trying to prevent the stolen base, credit a stolen base. Do not charge an error unless the wild throw permits the stealing runner to advance one or more extra bases, or permits another runner to advance, in which case credit the stolen base and charge one error to the catcher.

(c) When a runner, attempting to steal or after being picked off base, evades being put out in a run-down play and advances to the next base without the aid of an error, credit the runner with a stolen base. If another runner also advances on the play, credit both runners with stolen bases. If a runner advances while another runner, attempting to steal, evades being put out in a run-down play and returns safely, without the aid of an error, to the base originally occupied, credit a stolen base to the runner who advances.

(d) When a double or triple steal is attempted and one runner is thrown out before reaching and holding the base that runner is attempting to steal, no other runner shall be credited with the stolen base.

(e) When a runner is tagged out after oversliding a base, while attempting either to return to that base or to advance to the next base that runner shall not be credited with a stolen base.

(f) When in the scorer's judgment a runner attempting to steal is safe because of a muffed throw, do not credit a stolen base. Credit an assist to the fielder who made the throw; charge an error to the fielder who muffed the throw, and charge the runner with "Caught Stealing."

(g) No stolen base shall be scored when a runner advances solely because of the defensive team's indifference to the advance. Score as a fielder's choice.

CAUGHT STEALING

(h) A runner shall be charged as "Caught Stealing" if that runner is put out, or would have been put out by errorless play, when the runner:
1. Tries to steal.
2. Is picked off a base and tries to advance.
3. Overslides while stealing.
NOTE: Do not charge "Caught Stealing" unless the runner has an opportunity to be credited with a stolen base when the play starts.

SACRIFICES

10.09—

(a) Score a sacrifice bunt when, before two are out, the batter advances one or more runners with a bunt and is put out at first base, or would have been put out except for a fielding error.

(b) Score a sacrifice bunt when, before two are out, the fielders handle a bunted ball without error in an unsuccessful attempt to put out a preceding runner advancing one base.
EXCEPTION: When an attempt to turn a bunt into a putout of a preceding runner fails, and in the scorer's judgment perfect play would not have put out the batter at first base, the batter shall be credited with a one-base hit and not a sacrifice.

(c) Do not score a sacrifice bunt when any runner is put out attempting to advance one base on a bunt. Charge the batter with a time at bat.

(d) Do not score a sacrifice bunt when, in the judgment of the scorer, the batter is bunting primarily for a base hit and not for the purpose of advancing a runner or runners. Charge the batter with a time at bat.
NOTE: In applying the above rule, always give the batter the benefit of the doubt.

(e) Score a sacrifice fly when, before two are out, the batter hits a fly ball or a line drive handled by an outfielder which:
(1) is caught, and a runner scores after the catch, or
(2) is dropped, and a runner scores, if in the scorer's judgment the runner could have scored after the catch had the fly been caught.
NOTE: Score a sacrifice fly in accordance with 10.09 (d) (2) even though another runner is forced out by reason of the batter becoming a runner.

PUTOUTS

10.10—A putout shall be credited to each fielder who (1) catches a fly ball or a line drive, whether fair or foul; (2) catches a thrown ball which puts out a batter or runner, or 3) tags a runner when the runner is off the base to which that runner legally is entitled.

(a) Automatic putouts shall be credited to the catcher as follows:
(1) When the batter is called out for an illegally batted ball;
(2) When the batter is called out for bunting foul for the third strike (note exception in 10.17 (a) (2);
(3) When the batter is called out for being touched by that batter's own batted ball;
(4) When the batter is called out for interfering with the catcher;
(5) When the batter is called out for failing to bat in the proper turn (see 10.03 (d));
(6) When the batter is called out for refusing to touch first base after receiving a base on balls;
(7) When a runner is called out for refusing to advance from third base to home with the winning run.

(b) Other automatic putouts shall be credited as follows (credit no other assists on these plays except as specified):
(1) When a batter is called out on an Infield Fly which is not caught, credit the putout to the fielder who the scorer believes could have made the catch;
(2) When a runner is called out for being touched by a fair ball (including an Infield Fly), credit the putout to the fielder nearest the ball;
(3) When a runner is called out for running out of line to avoid being tagged, credit the putout to the fielder whom the runner avoided;
(4) When a runner is called out for passing another runner, credit the putout to the fielder nearest the point of passing;
(5) When a runner is called out for running the base in reverse order, credit the putout to the fielder covering the base the runner left in starting the reverse run;
(6) When a runner is called out for having interfered with a fielder, credit the putout to the fielder with whom the runner interfered, unless the fielder was in the act of throwing the ball when the interference occurred, in which case credit the putout to the fielder for whom the throw was intended, and credit an assist to the fielder whose throw was interfered with;
(7) When the batter-runner is called out because of interference by a preceding runner, as provided in Playing Rule 6.05 (m), credit the putout to the first baseman. If the fielder interfered with was in the act of throwing the ball, credit that fielder with an assist, but credit only one assist on any one play under the provisions of 10.10(b) (6) and (7).

ASSISTS

10.11—An assist shall be credited to each fielder who throws or deflects a batted or thrown ball in such a way that a putout results, or would have resulted except for a subsequent error by a fielder. Only one assist and no more shall be credited to each fielder who throws or deflects the ball in a rundown play which results in a putout, or would have resulted in a putout, except for a subsequent error.
NOTE: Mere ineffective contact with the ball shall not be considered an assist. "Deflect" shall mean to slow down or change the direction of the ball and thereby effectively assist in putting out a batter or runner.

(a) Credit an assist to each fielder who throws or deflects the ball during a play which results in a runner being called out for interference, or for running out of line.

(b) Do not credit an assist to the pitcher for a strikeout.
EXCEPTION: Credit an assist if the pitcher fields an uncaught third strike and makes a throw which results in a putout.

(c) Do not credit an assist to the pitcher when, as the result of a legal pitch received by the catcher a runner is put out, as when the catcher picks a runner off base, throws out a runner trying to steal, or tags a runner trying to score.

(d) Do not credit an assist to a fielder whose wild throw permits a runner to advance, even though the runner subsequently is put out as result of continuous play. A play which follows a misplay (whether or not it is an error) is a new play, and the fielder making any misplay shall not be credited with an assist unless that fielder takes part in a new play.

DOUBLE PLAYS — TRIPLE PLAYS

10.12—Credit participation in the double play or triple play to each fielder who earns a putout or an assist when two or three players are put out between the time a pitch is delivered and the time the ball next becomes dead or is next in possession of the pitcher in pitching position, unless an error or misplay intervenes between putouts.
NOTE: Credit the double play or triple play also if an appeal play after the ball is in possession of the pitcher results in an additional putout.

ERRORS

10.13—An error shall be charged for each misplay (fumble, muff or wild throw) which prolongs the time at bat of a batter or which prolongs the life of a runner, or which permits a runner to advance one or more bases.
NOTE: (1) Slow handling of the ball which does not involve mechanical misplay shall not be construed as an error.

NOTE: (2) It is not necessary that the fielder touch the ball to be charged with an error. If a ground ball goes through a fielder's legs or a pop fly falls untouched and in the scorer's judgment the fielder could have handled the ball with ordinary effort, an error shall be charged.
NOTE: (3) Mental mistakes or misjudgments are not to be scored as errors unless specifically covered in the rules.

(a) An error shall be charged against any fielder when that fielder muffs a foul fly to prolong the time at bat of a batter, whether the batter subsequently reaches first base or is put out.

(b) An error shall be charged against any fielder when that fielder catches a thrown ball or a ground ball in time to put out the batter-runner and fails to tag first base or the batter-runner.

(c) An error shall be charged against any fielder when that fielder catches a thrown ball or a ground ball in time to put out any runner on a force play and fails to tag the base or the runner.

(d) (1) An error shall be charged against any fielder whose wild throw permits a runner to reach a base safely, when in the scorer's judgment a good throw would have put out the runner.
EXCEPTION: No error shall be charged under this section if the wild throw is made attempting to prevent a stolen base.
(2) An error shall be charged against any fielder whose wild throw in attempting to prevent a runner's advance permits that runner or any other runner to advance one or more bases beyond the base that would have been reached had the throw not been wild.
(3) An error shall be charged against any fielder whose throw takes an unnatural bounce or touches a base or the pitcher's plate, or touches a runner, a fielder or an umpire, thereby permitting any runner to advance.
NOTE: Apply this rule even when it appears to be an injustice to a fielder whose throw was accurate. Every base advanced by a runner must be accounted for.
(4) Charge only one error on any wild throw, regardless of the number of bases advanced by one or more runners.

(e) An error shall be charged against any fielder whose failure to stop, or try to stop, an accurately thrown ball permits a runner to advance, providing there was occasion for the throw. If such throw be made to second base, the scorer shall determine whether it was the duty of the second baseman or the shortstop to stop the ball, and an error shall be charged to the negligent player.
NOTE: If in the scorer's judgment there was no occasion for the throw, an error shall be charged to the fielder who threw the ball.

(f) When an umpire awards the batter or any runner or runners one or more bases because of interference or obstruction, charge the fielder who committed the interference or obstruction with one error, no matter how many bases the batter, or runner or runners, may be advanced.
NOTE: Do not charge an error if obstruction does not change the play in the opinion of the scorer.

10.14—No error shall be charged in the following cases:

(a) No error shall be charged against the catcher when, after receiving the pitch, that catcher makes a wild throw attempting to prevent a stolen base, unless the wild throw permits the stealing runner to advance one or more bases.

(b) No error shall be charged against any fielder who makes a wild throw if in the scorer's judgment the runner would not have been put out with ordinary effort by a good throw, unless such wild throw permits any runner to advance beyond the base that runner would have reached had the throw not been wild.

(c) No error shall be charged against any fielder when that fielder makes a wild throw in attempting to complete a double play or triple play, unless such wild throw enables any runner to advance beyond the base that runner would have reached had the throw not been wild.

NOTE: When a fielder muffs a thrown ball, which, if held, would have completed a double play or triple play, charge an error to the fielder who drops the ball and credit an assist to the fielder who made the throw.

(d) No error shall be charged against any fielder when, after fumbling a ground ball or dropping a fly ball, a line drive or a thrown ball, the fielder recovers the ball in time to force out a runner at any base.

(e) No error shall be charged against any fielder who permits a foul fly to fall safe with a runner on third base before two are out, if in the scorer's judgment the fielder deliberately refuses the catch in order that the runner on third shall not score after the catch.

(f) Because the pitcher and catcher handle the ball much more than other fielders, certain misplays on pitched balls are defined in Rule 10.15 as wild pitches and passed balls. No error shall be charged when a wild pitch or passed ball is scored.
   (1) No error shall be charged when the batter is awarded first base on four called balls or because that batter was touched by a pitched ball, or when the batter reaches first base as the result of a wild pitch or passed ball.
      (i) When the third strike is a wild pitch, score a strikeout and a wild pitch;
      (ii) When the third strike is a passed ball, score a strikeout and a passed ball.
   (2) No error shall be charged when a runner or runners advance as the result of a passed ball, a wild pitch or a balk.
      (i) When the fourth called ball is a wild pitch or a passed ball, and as a result (a) the batter-runner advances to a base beyond first base; (b) any runner forced to advance by the base on balls advances more than one base, or (c) any runner, not forced to advance, advances one or more bases, score the base on balls, and also the wild pitch or passed ball, as the case may be;
      (ii) When the catcher recovers the ball after a wild pitch or passed ball on the third strike the batter is out, but another runner or runners advance, score the strikeout, the putouts and assists, if any, and credit the advance of the other runner or runners as having been made on the play.

WILD PITCHES — PASSED BALLS

10.15—
(a) A wild pitch shall be charged when a legally delivered ball is so high, or so wide, or so low that the catcher does not stop and control the ball by ordinary effort, thereby permitting a runner or runners to advance.
   (1) A wild pitch shall be charged when a legally delivered ball touches the ground before reaching home plate and is not handled by the catcher, permitting a runner or runners to advance.

(b) A catcher shall be charged with a passed ball when failing to hold or to control a legally pitched ball which should have been held or controlled with ordinary effort, thereby permitting a runner or runners to advance.

BASES ON BALLS

10.16—A base on balls shall be scored whenever a batter is awarded first base because of four balls having been pitched outside the strike zone, but when the fourth such ball touches the batter it shall be scored as a "Hit Batter" (see 10.18 (h) for procedure when more than one pitcher is involved in giving a base on balls.

(a) If a batter awarded a base on balls is called out for refusing the advance to first base, do not credit the base on balls. Charge a time at bat.

STRIKEOUTS

10.17—
(a) A strikeout shall be scored whenever:
   (1) A batter is put out by a third strike caught or not caught by the catcher;
   (2) A batter bunts foul on the third strike.
      EXCEPTION: If such bunt on third strike results in a foul fly, caught by a fielder, do not score a strikeout. Credit the fielder who catches such foul fly with a putout.

(b) When the batter leaves the game with two strikes and the substitute batter completes a strikeout, charge the strikeout and the time at bat to the first batter. If the substitute batter completes the turn at bat in any other manner, score the action as having been that of the substitute batter.

EARNED RUNS

10.18—An earned run is a run for which the pitcher is held accountable. In determining earned runs, the inning should be reconstructed without the errors and passed balls, and the benefit of the doubt should always be given to the pitcher in determining which bases would have been reached by errorless play.

(a) An earned run shall be charged every time a runner reaches home base by the aid of safe hits, sacrifice bunts, a sacrifice fly, stolen bases, putouts, fielder's choices, bases on balls, hit batters, balks or wild pitches before fielding chances have been offered to put out the offensive team. For the purpose of this rule, a defensive interference penalty shall be construed as a fielding chance.
   (1) A wild pitch is solely the pitcher's fault, and contributes to an earned run just as a base on balls or a balk.

(b) No run shall be earned when scored by a runner who reaches first base (1) on a hit or otherwise after that batter's time at bat is prolonged by a muffed foul fly; (2) because of interference or obstruction, or (3) because of any fielding error.

(c) No run shall be earned when scored by a runner whose life is prolonged by an error, if such runner would have been put out by errorless play.

(d) No run shall be earned when the runner's advance is aided by an error, a passed ball, or defensive interference or obstruction, if the scorer judges that the run would not have scored without the aid of such misplay.

(e) Any error by a pitcher is treated exactly the same as an error by any other fielder in computing earned runs.

(f) Whenever a fielding error occurs, the pitcher shall be given the benefit of the doubt in determining to which bases any runners would have advanced had the fielding of the defensive team been errorless.

(g) When pitchers are changed during an inning, the relief pitcher shall not be charged with any run (earned or unearned) scored by a runner who was on base at the time the relief pitcher entered the game, nor for runs scored by any runner left on base by the preceding pitcher.
   NOTE: It is the intent of this rule to charge each pitcher with their number of runners put on base, rather than with the individual runners. When a pitcher puts runners on base and is relieved, that pitcher shall be charged with all runs subsequently scored up to and including the number of runners left on base when said pitcher left the game, unless such runners are put out without action by the batter, i.e. caught stealing, picked off base, or called out for interference when a batter-runner does not reach first base on the play.
   EXAMPLES:
    1. P1 walks A and is relieved by P2. B grounds out, sending A to second, C flies out. D singles, scoring A. Charge run to P1.
    2. P1 walks A and is relieved by P2. B forces A at second. C grounds out sending B to second. D singles, scoring B. Charge run to P1.
    3. P1 walks A and is relieved by P2. B singles, sending A to third. C grounds to short and A is out at home. B going to second. D flies out. E singles, scoring B. Charge run to P1.
    4. P1 walks A and is relieved by P2. B walks. C flies out. A is picked off second, D doubles, scoring B from first. Charge run to P2.

    5. P1 walks A and is relieved by P2. P2 walks B and is relieved by P3. C forces A at third. D forces B at third. E hits home run, scoring three runs. Charge one run to P1, one run to P2 and one run to P3.
    6. P1 walks A and is relieved by P2. P2 walks B. C singles, filling the bases. D forces A at home. E singles scoring B and C. Charge one run to P1 and one run to P2.

(h) A relief pitcher shall not be held accountable when the first batter to whom that relief pitcher pitches reaches first base on four called balls if such batter has a decided advantage in the ball and strike count when pitchers are changed.
   (1) If, when pitchers are changed, the count is
      2 balls, no strike,
      2 balls, 1 strike,
      3 balls, no strike,
      3 balls, 1 strike,
      3 balls, 2 strikes,
     and the batter gets a base on balls, charge that batter and the base on balls to the preceding pitcher, not to the relief pitcher.
   (2) Any other action by such batter, such as reaching base on a hit, an error, a fielder's choice, a force-out, or being touched by a pitched ball, shall cause such a batter to be charged to the relief pitcher.
      NOTE: The provisions of 10.18 (h) (2) shall not be construed as affecting or conflicting with the provisions of 10.18 (g).
   (3) If, when pitchers are changed, the count is
      2 balls, 2 strikes,
      1 ball, 2 strikes,
      1 ball, 1 strike,
      1 ball, no strike,
      no ball, 2 strikes,
      no ball, 1 strike,
    charge that batter and that batter's action to the relief pitcher.

(i) When pitchers are changed during an inning, the relief pitcher shall not have the benefit of previous chances for outs, not accepted in determining earned runs.
   NOTE: It is the intent of this rule to prevent relief pitchers from not being charged with earned runs for which they are solely responsible.
   EXAMPLES:
    1. With two putout, P1 walks A. B reaches base on an error. P2 relieves P1. C hits home run, scoring three runs. Charge two unearned runs to P1, one earned run to P2.
    2. With two out, P1 walks A and B and is relieved by P2. C reaches base on an error. D hits home run, scoring four runs. Charge two unearned runs to P1, two unearned runs to P2.
    3. With none out, P1 walks A. B reaches base on an error. P2 relieves P1: C hits home run, scoring three runs. D and E strike out. F reaches base on an error. G hits home run, scoring two runs. Charge two runs, one earned, to P1. Charge three runs, two earned, to P2.

WINNING AND LOSING PITCHER

10.19—
(a) Credit the starting pitcher with a game won only if that pitcher has pitched at least four complete innings and that pitcher's team not only is in the lead when said pitcher is replaced but remains in the lead the remainder of the game.

(b) The "must pitch four complete innings" rule in respect to the starting pitcher shall be in effect for all games of six or more innings. In a five-inning game, credit the starting pitcher with a game won only if that pitcher has pitched at least four complete innings and that pitcher's team not only is in the lead when said pitcher is replaced but remains in the lead the remainder of the game.

(c) When the starting pitcher cannot be credited with the victory because of the provisions of 10.19 (a) or (b) and more than one relief pitcher is used, the victory shall be awarded on the following basis:
   (1) When, during the tenure of the starting pitcher, the winning team assumes the lead and maintains it to the finish of the game, credit the victory to the relief pitcher judged by the scorer to have been the most effective;
   (2) Whenever the score is tied the game becomes a new contest insofar as the winning and losing pitcher is concerned;
   (3) Once the opposing team assumes the lead all pitchers who have pitched up to that point are excluded from being credited with the victory except that if the pitcher against whose pitching the opposing team gained the lead continues to pitch until that pitcher's team regains the lead, which it holds to the finish of the game, that pitcher shall be the winning pitcher.
   (4) Normally, the winning relief pitcher shall be the one who is the pitcher of record when the team assumes the lead and maintains it to the finish of the game.
      EXCEPTION: Do not credit a victory to relief pitcher who pitches briefly or ineffectively if a succeeding relief pitcher pitches effectively in helping to maintain the team in the lead. In such case, credit the succeeding relief pitcher with the victory.

(d) When a pitcher is removed for a substitute batter or substitute runner, all runs scored by the pitcher's team during the inning in which the pitcher is removed shall be credited to the pitcher's benefit in determining the pitcher of record when that pitcher's team assumes the lead.

(e) Regardless of how many innings the first pitcher has pitched, that pitcher shall be charged with the loss of the game if replaced when the team is behind in the score, or falls behind because of runs charged to that pitcher after said pitcher is replaced, and that pitcher's team thereafter fails either to tie the score or gain the lead.

(f) No pitcher shall be credited with pitching a shutout unless that pitcher pitches the complete game, or unless said pitcher enters the game with none out before the opposing team has scored in the first inning, puts out the side without a run scoring, and pitches all the rest of the game. When two or more pitchers combine to pitch a shutout, a notation to that effect should be included in the league's official pitching records.

SAVES FOR RELIEF PITCHES

10.20—
(a) Credit a save to a relief pitcher who enters a game with that relief pitcher's team in the lead if the relief pitcher holds the lead the remainder of the game, provided that relief pitcher is not credited with the victory.

(b) A relief pitcher cannot be credited with a save if that relief pitcher does not finish the game unless the relief pitcher is removed for a pinch-hitter or pinch-runner.

(c) When more than one relief pitcher qualifies for a save under the provisions of this rule, credit the save to the relief pitcher judged by the scorer to have been the most effective. Only one save can be credited in any game.

DETERMINING PERCENTAGE RECORDS

10.21—To compute:
(a) Percentage of games won and lost, divide the number of games won by the total games won and lost;
(b) Batting average, divide the total number of safe hits (not the total bases on hits) by the total times at bat, as defined in 10.02 (a);
(c) Slugging percentage, divide the total bases of all safe hits by the total times at bat, as defined in 10.02 (a);
(d) Fielding average, divide the total putouts and assists by the total of putouts, assists and errors;
(e) Pitcher's earned-run average, multiply the total earned runs charged against said pitcher by six, and divide the result by the total number of innings the pitcher pitched.